The Sexual Side of Love

The Sexual Side of Love

by Maureen Green

Aldus Books London

Series Coordinator: John Mason
Design Director: Guenther Radtke
Picture Editor: Peter Cook
Editor: Mary Senechal
Copy Editor: Mitzi Bales
Research: Elizabeth Lake
         Lynette Trotter
Consultants: Beppie Harrison
          Jo Sandilands

Contents

This is a good time to be a woman. Not for centuries have women been allowed to fulfill themselves sexually as they are today, and probably never before have they been surrounded with so much encouragement to do so. But this modern emphasis on standards, goals, and rules for sexual happiness may all too easily leave a woman with the feeling that her sexual life must be inadequate. That is why this book aims to set sexual love in its true context as an integral part of each woman's life. It gives a frank but sensible, woman's-eye view of the emotional as well as the physical aspects of sexual love. And above all, it sets out to help any woman who wishes it to achieve greater fulfillment for herself and her partner within their own individual sexual relationship.

Love and Lovers

The desire to love and to be loved is one of the most universal feelings on earth. Two people in love seem to spell total happiness.

Below: for Western culture, Adam and Eve started it all in their Biblical paradise.

Above: Romeo and Juliet are among the most famous lovers in literature. Their tragic tale of true love that did not run smooth has been popular since Shakespeare wrote it.

Right: an early 20th-century postcard, made in Italy, gives a highly romantic picture of love. It shows two lovers totally enveloped in their own high leaping flames of passion.

Left: the happy ending comes for a couple after the tangles and misunderstandings of a typical cartoonized love story. Much Pop art of the 1960's satirized comic book drawings.

Below: modern lovers often look for a different definition of love, but their goal in love remains the same. It is to create a deep and lasting relationship between two people.

Our Sensual Ancestors

The pursuit of sensual pleasure has a long history, going many many centuries back.

Right: this 17th-century painting depicts the Romans at a wild and orgiastic party.

Below: ancient Indian temyle sculpture was often remarkably erotic in theme and design.

Below: the world-famous artist, Peter Paul Rubens (1577-1640) depicted a brutal rape scene in this powerful, realistic oil painting.

Above: a "stolen kiss," painted in fresco, shows how lusty Renaissance Italians were.

Below: mixed communal bathing was both popular and widespread in the Middle Ages.

Below left: a medieval chastity belt, made of heavy metal and locked into place between the legs, looks like a torture instrument.

The "Other Woman" in History

To our ancestors, a wife's role was that of mother and hostess, while it was the "other woman"—a man's mistress—who provided fun, companionship, and sensual pleasure.

Above: in Moslem countries, the picture was different. Wealthy men could have a harem of wives well versed in the art of erotic delight.

Right: for lovers of riotous living, the taverns and brothels of 18th-century Europe provided unlimited female society—at a price.

Above right: Nell Gwyn, mistress of King Charles II of England, delighted the people with her broad wit and unaffected manners.

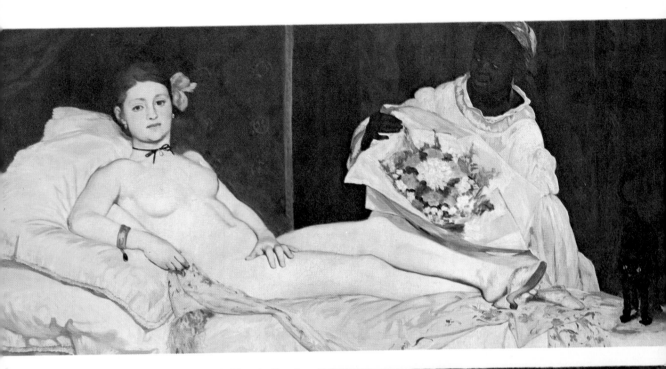

Above: Edouard Manet scandalized Paris society by using a girl of the streets as a model.

Right: Madame de Pompadour, brilliant mistress of King Louis XV of France, used her position to play a powerful role in politics.

The Victorian Reaction

In the Victorian era, sex became a taboo subject, hedged about with guilt and fear. Sexual feelings were considered too shameful for "decent" women even to know about.

Below: when sexual contact between lovers was denied, an over-sentimentalized view of romantic love became the order of the day.

Above: the Victorian family revolved around the stern figure of Papa, who jealously guarded the virtue of his wife and daughters.

Below: early Christian teaching reinforced the Victorian view that sex is sinful unless it be only for procreation within marriage.

Left: for all his apparent moral rectitude, the 19th-century husband was not above temptation. Beneath the respectable facade of Victorian society, prostitution flourished.

Above: the insistence on female chastity was all too easily overlooked when it came to working class girls, many of whom were driven to prostitution by poverty and hunger.

13

Love and Sex Today

After the stern moral reaction of the Victorian era, the wheel has spun well around toward freedom again. Less hampered by rules that seek to govern sexual behavior, today's men and women can exercise freedom of choice.

Below and below right: with the invention of the Pill, and the removal of the danger of unwanted pregnancy, the greatest barrier to full sexual freedom has disappeared at last.

Bottom right: in today's less inhibited atmosphere, men and women are demanding the right to love as they choose. This girl is demonstrating in New York for "gay" lib.

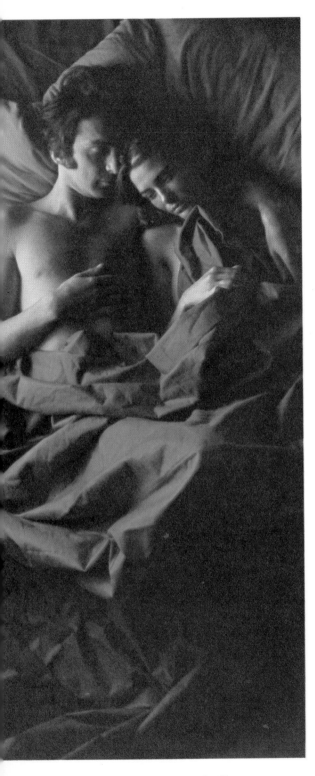

Below: with our new freedom, it is our concept of marriage that has undergone the most revolutionary change. We realize that marriage is not the only future for women, but for those of us who do marry, it will be the deepest and most fulfilling relationship we ever hope to achieve. Such a relationship should develop as we do, growing and strengthening all the years of our lives.

Above: now that sexual feelings are no longer stifled in the mists of Victorian Romanticism, and personal relationships are openly discussed, everyone recognizes the important part that sex plays in love.

15

The Freedom to Love

1

This is the best of all times to be a woman. It is not just that women today can do many things that in the past were reserved for men. It is also that today women are encouraged to enjoy doing the things that have always been part of being a woman. For the first time, all women are being offered the chance to find out about, to develop, and to experience to the full their capacity for love and sex.

It is little short of a revolution. For the majority of women it is much more important than the revolutions that have allowed them to vote and work. Modern women might not agree totally with the famous poet Lord Byron, that:

"Love's of man's life a thing apart,
Tis women's whole existence."

But they would agree that sensual love— the feelings and physical experiences that make up the exhilarations of love affairs and the pleasures of marriage—are a central part of a woman's world. Her creativity, her imagination, her hope is frequently expressed through sensual love.

For much of the past women have been more cut off from love than many can imagine. In many civilizations women were expected to marry, as virgins, partners who were chosen for them—and any later escape into adultery was strictly punished. In such circumstances sensual love was a forbidden experience. In more recent generations, in the times of our grandmothers, women were allowed to "fall in love" and choose their marriage partners, and marriage was the center of their lives. But physical love was looked upon as an unmentionable animal instinct. Most women submitted to their husbands out of a sense of duty and a desire for children. They were encouraged to think that a lady could not possibly *enjoy* sex. Instead they prided themselves on being above such things.

Today, this will not do. Modern science has observed both the minds and bodies of men and women, and assures us that the sexual instinct is not only basic to our survival as a species, but is also basic to our acceptance and enjoyment of life as individuals. We need the physical and emotional experiences of sex to live healthy lives. Psychologists tell us they have traced hysterical nervous and mental diseases to the strain of repressed and confused sexual feelings. The most recent scientific researches have observed men and women during intercourse in a laboratory, and give us for the first time complete knowledge of what our bodies can achieve during sexual excitement and satisfaction. We are all surrounded with so much information about sex that we may be forgiven for thinking that the Twentieth Century discovered it. The greatest fears surrounding sex throughout history—the fears of producing unwanted children or of contracting fatal and crippling venereal disease—have been solved in our century by modern medicine. Everything combines to give us the go-ahead. In theory we have reached the ultimate heights of sexual happiness.

Yet in practice, we have to agree that the

Today's greater understanding of human sexuality has given men and women the freedom to approach the sexual side of their relationship without fear or shame. Together, they can explore the joys of an equal partnership in which sex is the deepest and most rewarding expression of their love.

promised land of total sexual contentment has not yet arrived. Probably it never will. Sex is too vital, too interesting, and too personal not to arouse controversy. In fact, some of the conflicts that should have disappeared, and many unnecessary anxieties and inhibitions, are still with us. The popularity of marriage manuals and books of sex manners shows that many people still are very uncertain as to how they are expected to behave. Because the sexual expectations and standards of women have changed most of all, they are at the center of current confusion. Making love to uncertain women is not reassuring for men either.

Today, most women feel that sex is one more aspect of life that they must make a success of. Though they might not phrase it in quite the same way, many women today long to be what "J", author of *The Sensuous Woman,* describes as "that perfect combination of a lady in the living room and a marvelous bitch in bed." The nightmare of modern women is that they might appear, to themselves or their men, only as a bitch.

And it is not a nightmare without some foundation. In the past, men have often found it difficult to reconcile in their minds the idea of the noble woman who is their wife and the mother of their children, with the vital animal who could give them maximum sexual pleasure. They found it easier, if very cruel, to insist that there were "two kinds of women"—those that a man marries and those that he plays with. Though few women now would say, "I'm not that kind of girl", this statement was thought to be a valid way to explain to a man why you would not go to bed with him until very recently. Today, it is more accepted that every healthy woman is "that kind of girl" in her sex life. But is it totally accepted?

The great pioneer of psychology, Sigmund Freud, maintained that in every civilized man the conflict is always there: an inhibition in approaching a "nice" woman who resembles his image of his mother and represents what he desires emotionally in a

wife, and a freedom in approaching a bar girl or some other woman who will not have the power over him that these family women have. A man has, until recently, been reluctant to invest the same woman with the power of both wife and lover.

If this is how complicated it is for men, naturally it is more difficult for the woman who lives the part. Though the marriage manuals, and her husband, may encourage her to "complete abandon in the bedroom", she may worry about whether a nice girl really does show such abandon—and it may be impossible for her to do so. The only cure for this is by living through it. Only by proving to herself and her husband that she can be both women—an unthinking creature who is all body and senses at one time, and a rational person who can handle his

Left: this scene from a French tapestry, made for a wedding in the late 1400's, illustrates the traditional emphasis on chastity before marriage. According to medieval legend, the unicorn (a symbol of virility and strength) could only be captured if a virgin lured it to put its head in her lap, thus stressing the power of purity and symbolizing the sexual awakening of the virgin bride by her husband.

Right: the white wedding dress of today's bride is also a symbol of virginity. Now, however, chastity before marriage is becoming more a matter of individual choice. And while some girls prefer to remain virgins until they are married, over half the brides who go to the altar in white are already sexually experienced.

budget at another—will they be more able to relax over her switches in role.

Besides being invited to abandon herself in sexual passion, a woman is also encouraged by today's sex manuals to be an equal partner in the sex act, and to sometimes be the initiator and aggressor. But does she dare? She probably doesn't feel like an aggressor. In most other areas of their life together, she sees her husband or lover as the dominant one, the leader. How can she reverse this in bed? The answer is that she cannot behave totally differently in bed. It is only when a woman sees herself as sometimes being the initiator in daily life—and equal to her husband in all aspects of living—that she can convincingly play a leader's role in her lovemaking. No girl who is timid about her general approach to living can change enough to assert herself in bed.

A woman's whole status in the world outside is inextricably part of her sex life. The doubts that surround her status are vividly illustrated in the many discussions that have poured out in books, speeches, and articles about the contraceptive pill.

Although much of the discussion was supposed to be about the medical aspects, such as safety and reliability, a great deal of moral questioning also arose—not because this was contraception, but because this was contraception *for women*. For many years easily available contraception had been the

20

Left: a dutiful daughter sits meekly by while her parents argue the practical details of her marriage contract. Up until the last century, love was seldom a factor in marriage. Most marriages were arranged, as they still are in parts of the East.

Right: today, women in the West are free to choose their own partners and to fall in love before they marry. Modern marriages are rarely made for economic reasons, but rather for love and companionship.

prerogative of men. Though it frequently did not work, and led to accidental pregnancies, far less fuss was made. But with women obtaining contraceptives, moral mayhem was forecast. Some authorities, usually male, predicted that giving women control of contraception would make for a promiscuous society—though it is generally accepted that women are less promiscuous than men.

The dire forecasts have not come true. In fact, many surveys support the view that the Pill has a stabilizing effect. For example, it has helped married women to relax and enjoy their lovemaking without fear of producing a fourth or fifth child. It has in many cases stabilized the lives of young girls who take it, allowing them to continue a serious relationship with one man.

Lucy was a young secretary when she first met Joe at a party. After they had been seeing each other for three months, they felt that they were in love. Joe began to persuade her that they should make love to each other completely. Lucy was very

reluctant. It was not so much that she was still a virgin and afraid of beginning sexual experience. It was more that she was terrified of getting pregnant, and knew nothing about contraception. Gradually she confided this to Joe. Very sensibly, he encouraged her to go to a birth control clinic and enquire about taking the Pill. He also promised to split the cost of the

prescription with her. On this basis, Lucy began taking the Pill. She and Joe continued their relationship in peace of mind. Later, when they married, their early habit of cooperation and sharing helped them with planning other aspects of their life together.

This kind of thing now happens so frequently that social workers wryly comment: "the Pill has replaced the diamond

Men have often found it difficult to see in the same woman the virtues traditionally expected of a wife and mother, and the sexual passion of a lover. For women, too, it is not always easy to reconcile the responsibilities of motherhood and of running a home with the relaxation and abandonment necessary to pleasurable love making.

ring as an engagement symbol." Women have shown that given the responsibility for "protection", they can use it responsibly.

The double standard—the custom of setting a strict standard of sexual behavior for women while allowing total sexual freedom for men—has not totally disappeared. Modern contraception is the one thing that might finally banish it. The Pill removes the centuries-old reason why parents feel it best to "lock up their daughters." In the past, the result of every experience of sex could be pregnancy, so girls were carefully chaperoned and guarded to prevent the possibility of motherhood before marriage. Today, a girl may well collect emotional scars from an unhappy love affair, but at least she need not have an unwanted child.

Another effect of completely efficient contraception is the change in emphasis on the guarantee of paternity. Fatherhood is not a readily recognized biological fact, like motherhood. Many primitive tribes, in fact, never comprehended the man's role in conception, and when they were first told of it by Christian missionaries, refused to believe it. Many anthropologists maintain that, because of this indifference to paternity, relations between men and women are very free and unstrained in primitive life. In more advanced civilizations, however, once a man's role in begetting children was recognized, his longing for legitimate offspring, his hopes for immortality in the form of his own flesh and blood, his desire to pass on property to his own blood—all this has led men to be repressive in their attitude to women. A woman's chastity was the only guarantee a man had that her children were his. Her abstention from sex with anyone but him became, therefore, a matter of the greatest importance to him. Sexual jealously in the male was reinforced by strong social pressures. "The discovery of fatherhood led to the subjection of women as the only means of securing their virtue", says the

Unlike the carefully chaperoned courting couples of the past, young people today have the chance to be alone together and to decide for themselves what restraints—if any—they wish to put on their relationship.

Left: in the past, the desire for heirs to carry on a man's name and inherit his property was a prime reason for marriage. Husbands insisted on the absolute fidelity of their wives as a guarantee of their paternity.

Center and right: children are no longer a duty imposed by nature and society, and in the smaller family of today, men can play a greater part in the upbringing of their sons and daughters.

philosopher Bertrand Russell. . . . "Love as a relation between men and women was ruined by the desire to make sure of the legitimacy of the children."

At the root of greater freedom of women today is the fact that, with contraception, men no longer have to bully women into total fidelity. It does not have to matter to a father or a husband, in the way that it did to a Victorian father or husband, that the women in his family were "virtuous."

However, there are other mental worries that we think we have overcome, but that we have probably simply driven into our unconscious. Very few men or women today would admit that they think sex is sinful, but because the tradition in our civilization that sex is impure is so deep, it is unlikely that we have reversed it completely in the last two generations. Though a woman may well laugh today if teased by her lover that she is a "wicked, wicked girl", the idea of the sinfulness of sex was no laughing matter in the past. The link of sex to sin was invented by men—as all the world's great religions were—so sinful sex was linked to woman and interwoven with religious teachings.

Although it is too familiar a story to need repeating, the idea of the early Christians (not of Christ himself) about the sins of the flesh, and the need to mortify the flesh, have had a deep effect on all of western civilization. Christian churches today still contain services for the purification of women after childbirth, because this great event in a woman's life is seen as unclean. It is men who have organized religions declaring that all sin is represented by women. The original story of male buck-passing by Adam to Eve is one we all know from the Bible.

While most of this is behind us—and is part of the not-regretted past—just enough of it lingers to cause doubts in some women's minds about whether they really can enjoy using their sexual powers. Recent science may tell us that sex is good for us, but in our bones is the teaching of thousands of years that it is sin. Modern marriage manuals may invite women to pursue multiple orgasms, but buried in our systems

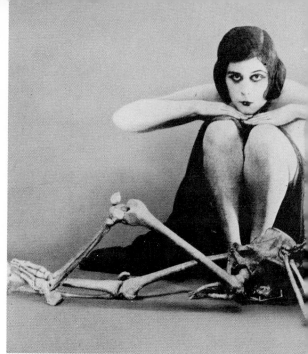

is the medieval teaching that sex was less of a sin if no pleasure was felt. Orgasm was thought to be the moment of greatest sin in the Middle Ages, the moment when men and women blot out reason and knowledge of God.

Not only religion, but also our whole hygiene-conscious western civilization work against full enjoyment of our sexuality. Our upbringing emphasizes neatness and tidiness, reasonableness and coolness. Sex is untidy, emotional, and abandoned. There is conflict between the virtues we are taught to admire, and the animal instincts that lead to the satisfactions of sensual love. Yet one of the reasons we value our sexuality so much is that it refuses to be tamed like the rest of our personality.

Even in the most compliant individuals, sex sometimes refuses to be of a like compliance. When mind and will have been disciplined to accept one decision—perhaps to marry someone not really loved—the body often refuses to follow through. Sex is the instinct that most resists being made to tell convenient lies. In modern times, when we often feel we are overcivilized and over-regimented, we value the lead that our sensuality gives in directing us to what we really want out of life.

But the changes in our civilization from

The portrayal of woman as an evil temptress, bent on luring pure men to doom, often expresses a deep-rooted belief in the sinfulness of sex. Left: traditional interpretations of the biblical story see Eve as an instrument of the devil who used sexuality to bring about the fall of man.

Above: Theda Bara, the first vamp of the silent films, is shown crouching over the skeleton of her latest male victim. Theda hit the screen in 1915 and her sensational career as the erotic vamp marked the beginning of the exploitation of sexy women in the movies.

Right: the seductiveness of the modern *femme fatale* continues to have wide appeal for men.

When a couple recognize the importance of sexual love to their health and happiness, they may seek additional knowledge to help them gain greater enjoyment from the sexual side of their marriage.

despising sex to valuing it have come so fast that women are often caught in contradictory situations. While their grandmothers were expected not to know anything about sex, women today feel that they are expected to know everything, perform marvelously, and aim at an expertise that was formerly reserved for the professional courtesan. What with the duties of homemaking and child rearing, the responsibilities of a job—or both at once—learning to be a marvelous lover can sometimes seem like one more frightening chore. Many modern sex manuals do nothing to help. They establish impossible standards, such as: that husband and wife should always achieve mutual and simultaneous orgasm, which the latest sex research has shown to be difficult at best; or that they should vary their lovemaking positions, including some which seem on paper to be both athletic and grotesque. Many books on sex make the reader feel depressed and inferior. A woman might feel like a beginning cook who, having just about learned to boil an egg, is asked to prepare a complicated gourmet meal.

It is important to remember that everyone's sex life, like every other part of her, is quite individual. No one has a perfect sex life, and no one ever had. We are not all equally talented sexually, nor equally ambitious. But there is always room for some improvement through additional knowledge, experience, and will. Since our sensuality is so central to happiness, even a minor improvement is well worthwhile. The main thing is to make a beginning toward greater sexual fulfillment.

30

Love, the Magic Ingredient
2

It is a sensation that we all know, but none of us can exactly describe. A million pop songs, and as many poems, have tried to sum it up, but there is always more to say. A man and a woman look at each other, and it begins: the age-old feeling of attraction. At first it may be something about their looks that draws their attention to each other. Later they may feel that they see so deeply into each other that they are not even aware of external appearance. But whatever it is—and experts have suggested it may depend on anything from recognizing the right neurosis to recognizing the right body smell—the rituals of courtship have begun. The imaginations of both are alive with fantasies of how marvelous and unique the other is. The bodies of both are tensed for the contests ahead.

At one and the same time, this is the start of the simple act of mating, and of one of the greatest emotional adventures in human experience. It is the beginning of the search for a partner to satisfy all our physical longings, conquer all our feelings of loneliness, and share our interests and our enthusiasms.

For a woman the search is an especially important one. Rooted in the act of mating itself is the enormous difference in the attitudes of men and women toward sex. The male animal is built for sexual hit-and-run. His desire is quickly aroused, his orgasm is intense, and within minutes he has fulfilled his role of fertilizing the female.

All the numerous sex manuals on sale today provide inadequate recipes for sexual happiness if they leave out the one magic and essential ingredient—love.

The female, on the other hand, is built for permanency. For her, desire is slow to rise, her orgasm is achieved more slowly and with greater difficulty, and every act of sex seems to hold a hint of her future as wife and mother in it. For her therefore, physical reactions are inextricably intertwined with her feelings toward the man as the possible father of her children, and with her assessment of his character as the possible provider of a secure life. Women have never been able to look on men simply as beautiful bodies. They fall in love with personality. Their approach has always been both more practical and more emotional. They look beyond the desirable body to the inner man, and always ask: could I rely on him? would he feel loyal to me? could I live with him for many years? does he love me deeply?

One school of thought on differences in the attitudes of the sexes holds that they are biologically based. Others argue against the biological point. But it is generally agreed that women have always taken the lead in trying to keep love, sex, and marriage together. Though the cynical may say, "women buy love with sex, and men buy sex with love", women in fact are most happy when the two are fused.

But the delicate balance between love and desire is not easy to achieve or to preserve. In some ways it was easier in the past for a man to have a wife and a mistress—one woman who washed his socks and another who gave him pleasure—and to feel differently about each. It is still often the easy way out today. The stresses and strains of life sometimes force a man into this attitude.

Take the case of David, for example. He is

now divorced, an attractive man of 44. For many years, he and his wife stayed together partly for the sake of their children, partly because money was tight, and partly because they had many interests in common. "But our sex life was always hopeless", David explains. "For the last ten years of our marriage, we had no sex at all." By the time the breakup came, David had become used to affairs with other women, and his wife had had many boyfriends, too. Because this continued for such a long time, David was left with a real problem after the divorce. "I'm so used to living with one person, and getting sex on the side, that I don't think I will ever be able to get love and sex together again".

David is not alone in this. Many individuals, and some whole societies in history, seem to have abandoned the struggle to satisfy mind and body together. Some people have always split love and sex, and just tried to make a go of one or the other. In the Victorian period, a majority concentrated almost exclusively on the tender feelings and fantasies that men and women have for and about each other. They made the mistake of assuming that sexual satisfaction would be automatic between two who feel deeply for each other. Moreover, women were supposed to be totally submissive in the sex act—which was considered base in itself—so they had little choice but to keep their minds on romantic love alone. The Victorians were reacting to the hard-hearted 18th century that had gone before. Then society concentrated on the worldly aspects of sex, on physical satisfactions, on bedroom intrigues intended to influence the court.

There seems to be a perpetual pendulum in human history between seeing love and sex in terms of mind, or in terms of body—a swing to and fro between puritanism and promiscuity.

But puritanism and promiscuity are in fact two sides of the same coin. They are both tricks to avoid loving as completely as human beings are capable of doing. The puritan cuts himself off from the potential power of sex; the promiscuous cut themselves off from the strong bonds of love. Stephen Vizinczey, author of the best-selling novel, *In Praise of Older Women*, says: "The whole puritan tradition—that sex was immoral—was really a heaven-sent excuse, a great escape from the whole irksome business. The other great escape is promiscuity, the refusal to feel, the refusal to

Left: in the permissive Regency era of early 19th-century England, a majority preferred the pursuit of pleasure to the less certain rewards of romantic love. Morals were lax, and promiscuity flourished.

Right: the Victorians went to the other extreme, exalting the tender emotions of romantic love at the expense of sensual pleasure. Sex was thought sinful and women were expected to deny sexual feelings.

involve your personality at the deepest level. You don't care about the other person. Sex is just sex."

Part of the great puritan escape is the long tradition of romantic love. Though romance has added so much enjoyment to the rituals of courtship, it is founded on a perverse game that is fun only if it is not pushed too far. The ideas of romance sprang up amidst the barbarism of the Dark Ages, when any man could have had any woman he wanted by force. To rescue their men and women from this brutishness, the knights and ladies of medieval France invented a game of unrequited love. A knight would pick out the wife of another man—a lady he was socially forbidden to seduce—and pay court to her, write her poems, send her flowers, wear her colors in tournaments. But he would never make love to her physically. She was above seduction. As a way of behavior it was mad, perverse, and, considering the age it sprang from, a totally unrealistic pastime. But it did disclose one very important aspect of sexual psychology. By denying physical satisfaction, men and women poured all their energies into their imaginations: feelings were heightened. In the end, a smile from the untouchable beloved produced ecstasies, a dropped glove became a treasure, a cold glance struck misery.

Perverse as it may have been, romance caught hold so deeply that western civilization has never gotten entirely rid of it. Every time some young man tortures himself with the idea that a woman will never have him, every time a man sends red roses, every time he opens a door for his female companion, he is still playing his part in the romantic cult. Many of the gestures today accepted as good manners between the sexes go back to the romantic tradition. And more besides. From this tradition, we have learned that frustrating desire a little fans the flames. It adds a delicious agony to sexual encounters.

The renowned philosopher Bertrand Russell wrote: "The belief in the immense

Above: all for the love of a lady, the gallant knight of old went forth to slay a dragon. By his bravery, he was thought to have proved the power of a pure, constant devotion that was the ideal of courtly love.

Below: the romantic tradition founded in the Middle Ages gave rise to an elaborate ritual of courtship that lasted for hundreds of years. Noble gentlemen were well versed in the rules of gallantry and courtesy that governed the game of romantic love.

Right: many of the gestures of love that we value today date back to the age of chivalry. When a man sends a woman red roses, for example, he is continuing a custom evolved by the knights and ladies of medieval France.

value of the lady is a psychological effect of the difficulty in obtaining her; and I think it may be laid down that when a man has no difficulty in obtaining a woman, his feeling towards her does not take the form of romantic love".

Today, the old fantasy of romance is almost dead. Relations between the sexes are direct and more honest, but, because of this, may sometimes seem a little less interesting. "All that business that used to go on about 'dreaming of the unobtainable' was very neurotic", says Sandy, a young woman who believes in and practices sexual freedom. "The knight on a white horse was just a con job. The first time I fell in love I had this strange illusion of seeing *his* face every time I rounded a corner. But we went to bed together and the vision stopped. I think my generation has lost the ability— or need—to delude itself with romantic bunk".

The sexual revolution of today has tried to overthrow the perversities of romantic love, and emphasizes instead the need for an active sexual life in maintaining health in mind and body. Rather than revel in unrequited love, a plunge into uninhibited sex is the advice of many today. Once again, a very important truth about sex lies behind the frequent excesses of permissiveness that we now witness. Sex is indeed a natural bodily appetite, and to the hungry any food is better than none. Sexual frustration is the cause of much mental illness, and possibly physical sickness as well, and therefore to be avoided.

Ever since Sigmund Freud began investigating the psychology of modern men and women—and he was working in the very repressed world of 19th-century Vienna—the enormously important role of sexuality in the mental and physical well-being of men and women has been propounded. But, perhaps because of the era in which he was working, Freud came to conclusions that many would not accept today. It is civilization that forces us to repress our sexual appetites, and gives rise to the distressing neuroses we

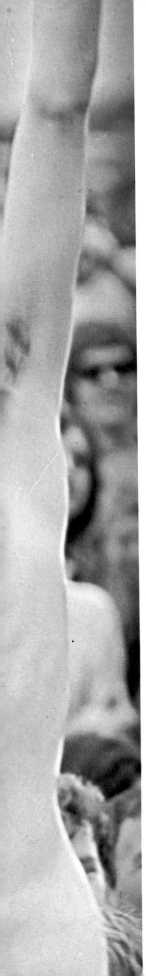

Left: youth has been the first to challenge conventional attitudes to sex, and to seize the opportunity for greater sexual freedom. This girl, dancing naked at a crowded pop festival like the one pictured above, makes her own emphatic stand against traditional inhibitions and taboos on the body.

see around us, says Freud, but these neuroses are the price we have to pay for the benefits of our culture.

One member of Freud's original circle refused to go along with this sad acceptance of the inevitability of neurosis as the price of civilization. His name was Wilhelm Reich. Reich maintained that sexual fulfillment was absolutely necessary to a healthy mind and body, and that sexual deprivation could result in anything from madness to cancer to social violence. He thought that destroying mankind's health was too high a price to pay for civilization. If necessary, civilization in his view must be overthrown, or at least radically changed. Faithfulness to one partner was to be abandoned as part of the change in society. Only by changing partners when need be could healthy sexual satisfaction be guaranteed, Reich felt. As a result of publishing his contrary theories in his book *The Function of the Orgasm*, Reich was expelled from his place among the great pioneers of psychology.

Yet it is the ideas of Reich that young revolutionaries have seized on today to justify their sexual revolution. "Make love not war", the students chant on college campuses, referring to his idea that sexual frustration builds up aggression. There is enough truth in these theories to make them persuasive propaganda. Most women know from their own experience how much more relaxed they feel, how much more easily they adjust to minor irritations of day-to-day life, how much kinder they can be when they are enjoying a good sexual life. When sex goes wrong, we also know from our own experience that edginess and nervous irritability can begin, and even build up into anger or slide into depression.

Because the 20th century is very concerned about avoiding the dangers of frustration, our whole attitude to sex has changed. Governments take the view that pornography should be dealt with lightly on a legal basis, since it probably solves as many problems for some frustrated individuals as it might cause for others. Homosexuality is treated with more tolerance. Age-old traditions, like the Roman Catholic rule of celibacy for its priesthood, are being challenged as unhealthy. Theatres permit shows that feature nudity and simulated sex, and magazines and books pour from the presses with advice on sexual technique and pleasure. Women's Lib has taken the hatchet to the image of the "fair lady" who spent most of her time being cold and cruel, and has pleaded with her to come down off her pedestal and lead an active—and equal—sex life.

The message has finally come across to almost everyone: sex is okay and good for you.

But where does this leave love? Peter and Caroline are two young students who are living together, after several sexual adventures with others. Caroline finds it "the most mature relationship that I have ever had." She explains: "Peter and I have been through the mill a bit in our separate lives but now perhaps we'll be able to build something on the ruins of what went before. We both now know that it isn't possible to be sexually faithful to one person forever. But sex isn't that important. I have been very jealous in the past but I think I have

The touch, the look, the nearness of that someone special makes the rest of the universe—and all its problems—fade away. A shared love makes young or old feel strong.

gotten over that. But I still think that I would like to have a child at some point in my life." In their mid-20's, Caroline and Peter have learned a lot about sex; but they are only beginners when it comes to love. As for the freedom that Caroline enjoys, some would still say it is only freedom to repress her natural longings for an exclusive love, and for the beginnings of maternal feelings.

Though many women may benefit from the present sexual permissiveness—and dare to take the occasional escape into an affair that they may need badly—others have found it a rocky and loveless road. Sex without love can provide a great physical release, but many find it incomplete. That incompleteness is felt in just the area most women respond to deeply: the emotions.

Elizabeth was 30 when her divorce finally came through. She was in a bitter mood. Her husband, whom she had adored when they were first married, had run off with another woman. Elizabeth could think of no reason to account for the collapse of her marriage, especially as the sexual part had always been good. She was a stunning looking woman too. What had gone wrong? She was totally unaware of how much stronger, livelier, and dominating she had been than her husband, and how he had sought refuge elsewhere when he realized that he could not compete. She had simply been conscious of an uneasiness in their marriage, a feeling that her husband seemed to take pleasure in sniping at her energies and abilities.

For a while, Elizabeth took advantage of her life as an attractive divorced woman to drift from one amiable affair to another. After a time, however, she met a widowed professor, a man some 20 years older than her. She fell deeply in love with him. This man, Stephen, was more than a match for her. He loved her immediately, but he had

Times may change and customs vary, but love's language is forever the same. Throughout the ages, lovers have known that a kiss or a touch can say more about the way they feel than a thousand words.

no intention of letting her outstrip him. Elizabeth learned for the first time to respect and listen to a man she loved. She began to learn from his experience and greater wisdom, and their sex life, although good, was not the only thing they shared. Her whole outlook on life changed. She became less self-centered, less frantic. Her natural warm-heartedness expanded. Both she and Stephen gained a new confidence in living because of their newly found love.

When they decided to marry, it was an inevitable formal step that recognized the something already there: their enormous commitment to each other. For Stephen, a lonely middle-age had been transformed by this attractive energetic woman. For Elizabeth, an unsettled and searching period had come to an end with genuine emotional security.

Sexual love, in these terms, is a way of communicating between a man and a woman in which feelings and physical reactions cannot be separated. Sex becomes a means of expression—the medium, and not the whole message.

For most women, sensual love becomes more worthwhile and more interesting in a long-term relationship, especially in the security of marriage. Because understanding and affection can be expressed in making love, arguments can be healed or celebrations can be given a special meaning in bed. At the same time, it is important for a woman to remember that what she feels can pass unnoticed if she doesn't know how to express her feelings sexually. If she is a fearful, clumsy, or ignorant lover, she will not be able to use the medium of sex to get her message across. This is one reason she will want to learn more of the skills of sensual love, and to make the ways of giving and receiving physical pleasure part of her language.

42

43

Love and Sex Inside Marriage
3

After the excitement and glamour of the wedding day, most brides face the start of married life with mixed emotions, especially if marriage provides their first real experience of sexual love.

Marriage is quite unlike anything else. For some women, it provides their first sexual partner; for others it provides their last. But whether this is the first venture into sexual life, or the final union that seems to promise stability, the important quality will be permanence. It is the notion of permanence that most endears marriage to women. It gives you time.

Time will influence everything about the relationship. It affects the choice of partner in the first place. A man and woman choose to marry in the hope that both of them will continue to be interesting to each other for up to half a century. They detect in each other some qualities that have hardly yet grown, but that promise to develop alongside characteristics of their own. They are, sometimes almost unconsciously, taking the long view of love.

They rarely take time into account in sex. At the beginning of almost every marriage, a couple makes love as though there is no tomorrow. They seem to have a perpetual hunger for each other, but if they are sexually inexperienced, they may not at first be able to abandon themselves completely. The young wife, in particular, may wonder and worry if some of their lovemaking could be destroying the picture her husband has of her. The more she allows her animal nature to emerge in bed, the more she tries to look crisp and fresh over breakfast.

Because newlyweds' desire for each other rises spontaneously at regular intervals, they have a good chance of overcoming any problems they may have. They may early detect a difference in sexual appetite. For

In marriage, a couple can afford to take a long term view of love. They have the time to explore each other's needs and to come to the closer sexual and emotional understanding that will enable their relationship to develop and deepen over the years.

example, he may want to make love more often than she does, and they may have to make some compromises that will not leave her exhausted nor him frustrated. This is a frequent occurence, but the situation usually smooths out in middle age when men lose sexual drive to a greater extent than women, and partners often find themselves more evenly matched.

Whatever the couple's problems, women feel that efforts to solve them stand a good chance of long-term rewards in the security of marriage. Women are, therefore, willing to invest everything they have.

In the safety of marriage, husband and wife explore each other's personalities, as they learn to feel safe to quarrel. They begin to realize that every disagreement does not carry a threat of separation because most tiffs can be made up by honest effort.

At the same time, they explore and experiment with each other's bodies to learn how to give and take the maximum pleasure, and to express their every mood. On a day that has been lighthearted and teasing, they may make love savagely on the kitchen floor. At the end of a day that has been tiring and depressing, they may make love gently and consolingly in the comfort of their bed. They can be flexible and tolerant, knowing they will be together for a long time.

But that knowledge, while it is the strength and essence of marriage, can also be a great problem. At the beginning, knowing that your husband has promised to spend his life with you is felt to be the greatest compliment and brings enormous emotional security and relaxation. Ten years later, you may have passed the subtle line between relying on someone and taking him totally for granted. At the beginning, knowing that you are able to make love to your husband whenever you want to is a stimulus. Ten years later there is a danger that the total availability of your partner may turn you off.

Marriage is made or marred by even

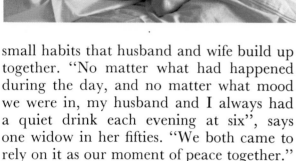

small habits that husband and wife build up together. "No matter what had happened during the day, and no matter what mood we were in, my husband and I always had a quiet drink each evening at six", says one widow in her fifties. "We both came to rely on it as our moment of peace together."

The sexual habits that are built up are of even greater importance. The best habit is variety. To always make love in one place or in one position, to always make love at a given time set aside for it can create deadly monotony. To make love frequently can give the appearance of great passion. But if it is a quick grappling by two tired people before they fall asleep, it can make sex become a minor event.

Every couple must work at solving the central problem of sexual monotony in marriage. The first popular handbook in this century to outline the need for sexual knowledge, and sexual skill, was *Ideal Marriage* by Theodore van de Velde. It was published in 1928, and it put all the blame on the husband for his lack of technique. "He does not know that there are numberless delicate differentiations and modifications of sexual pleasure that can banish the mechanical monotony of the too well-known from the marriage bed," wrote van de Velde. He then listed variations in positions for intercourse, and warned that "to the uninstructed man the only possible variation seems to be in the object of his efforts." Today, we are more likely to think that a woman, too, should aim to defeat sexual monotony in her marriage, and less likely to think that adultery is a simple reaction to sexual boredom.

"Never allow a quarrel to last overnight," is the advice of the French. Although it is not always easy to kiss and make up, bed is often the best place to put an end to a disagreement.

Though a sound knowledge of sexual technique is an important part of a woman's responsibility to her marriage (see Chapter 4), her state of mind, her continuing willingness to experiment, her capacity to be flexible is even more essential. If she still sees her marriage as an adventure, if she still expects the unexpected, she is in the right frame of mind.

Margaret, who is 27 and has been married for 5 years, took the right approach in overcoming the first sexual hurdle in her marriage. She found that she and her husband had gotten past the first frantic phase of sexuality in their marriage, when they seemed to need to make love almost daily. They learned that they enjoyed sex more in this second phase if they treated lovemaking a bit like a special occasion.

Above: for most women, pregnancy and the birth and care of a child provide the creative climax of their sensual lives. A pregnancy that is freely undertaken can be a unique and deeply joyful experience.

Right: some couples are disappointed in their hopes for a child. Continued failure to achieve a longed-for pregnancy can lead to anxieties and tensions that mar a couple's sexual relationship.

They did not get to the stage of formally making a date with each other to make love; but when Margaret noticed the right gleam in her husband's eye, she responded in kind. She would make sure that the children went to bed early, take a long luxurious bath, and prepare herself physically and mentally to enjoy herself. Her husband did the same. Sometimes they danced naked together; sometimes they drank together; but always they spent time and trouble *winning* each other. They never let their lovemaking become automatic.

Those who find it difficult to continue to be lovers when they are totally familiar with each other also often find it hard to make the transition from being in love to loving. They want ecstasy forever. The feeling of falling in love is one of the most exhilarating that we ever experience. What else is like that sudden feeling of contact, of breaking out from being a separate and lonely person, of uniting with someone else! It leads to an intense obsession with that other person, and a longing to know more and more about him; but though falling in love is what brings two people into marriage, it is only a temporary phase, and is bound to lead into something else. What it can lead to is loving, wanting, and working for the good of another person, not only for oneself. The possessiveness of love gives way to the ability to recognize that your husband is another person, an individual in his own right who is best loved and helped by relaxing and letting him be, rather than by grabbing and owning him.

For those who can reach it, this is the

most peaceful and satisfying state of all. Husband and wife are united, but are also separate and alive in their own right. Many people, however, cannot or do not wish to get to this stage. What they enjoy is the period of discovery and surrender. They pursue it again and again with different partners, often in affairs, but sometimes in multiple marriages.

For those who have come close enough to be able to let go a little, the rewards are great. The husband can grow and develop, moving into new phases of work or other interests. A wife can begin to take on the added love of their children without her husband fearing too jealously that he will be neglected. Certainly for the majority of women, the final climax of sex is childbirth; the whole cycle of pregnancy and care of a child brings her sensual life to a creative finish. In the past, many women resisted the idea of making love while they were pregnant, and postponed it for a while after childbirth. This was mainly because of puritanical ideas that it would not seem right. In most normal pregnancies, there can be no harm to the unborn child, and considerable benefit to the wife who stays internally supple if she continues a regular sex life.

For a substantial minority of couples, there is the problem of childlessness. One marriage in 20 is affected by some problem of infertility, and although few couples today would say that the sex act should always have conception as its final aim, most would find a sexual life that could not produce a pregnancy dispiriting. Such a disappointment can color a woman's whole attitude to her own and her husband's sexuality. If she wants children, a women should get medical advice the moment she suspects any infertility problem. She would certainly have doubts after trying for a year and failing to achieve pregnancy.

There are some marriages that are happy as duets, and do not need the addition of even one child. These are often marriages in which the husband and wife have some other highly absorbing interest in common, perhaps a business that they run together, or artistic or social ambitions. In any marriage, such a sharing of interests is a benefit. While a young married couple finds that the sexual attraction between them leads them to take notice of the interests and pursuits of their partners, the situation reverses itself. Later, it is the shared interests and enthusiasms that add fire to their sex life.

Can sex life remain only within the marriage at all times? Total fidelity to one partner has never been easy. For men it seems to go against their nature, and today there are added strains. Our whole culture places greater emphasis on sexual satisfaction, so that partners in temporary sexual doldrums become extremely self-conscious on this point. Our lives are more mobile, so that opportunities for casual affairs arise often not just for husbands, but also for wives. The strongest motive for total fidelity —the fear of bringing illegitimate offspring into the family—has lessened with better contraception. The fear of disease has largely disappeared, since the discovery of antibiotics. All that is left of the centuries-old pressures to remain totally faithful to each other is the wish and will to do so.

52

Left: today, when both
husband and wife are likely
to meet many other men and
women outside their home
circle—notably at work—
opportunities for a casual
affair may arise more
easily. According to a
recent survey, 75 per cent
of men and 40 per cent of
women have some kind of
sexual experience outside
their marriage.

53

The later years of marriage can mark the beginning of a new and enriched companionship, based on the sympathy, understanding, and shared experience of two people whose love has stood the test of time.

Sometimes, in the course of marriage that lasts much longer than that of our grandparents (our life expectation having increased by almost ten years), the will for fidelity falters. It is expecting a lot that it will not, yet most women find the discovery of adultery a shattering experience. If they find theater tickets in their husband's pocket and learn that he took some other woman out while he was away on a business trip; if they discover that he has made a pass at the wife of the friendly neighbors they see for drinks, women feel it as a dreadful blow to their self-esteem. In the last century, an adulterous husband would have been condemned as a faithless scoundrel. Today a wife is likely to blame herself for not being able to hold her man, even if she still resents and regrets his infidelity.

Her self-reproaches and self-doubts are understandable. It is the exclusive attachment of her husband that has made her feel an attractive and lovable woman, just as her love and interest has made him feel a whole man. Once that exclusive love is broken into, and damaged from outside, her confidence is shaken. "Maybe he doesn't love me? Maybe I am not lovable?" are questions that haunt her for a while. Her whole emotional security is undermined. The efforts she has made in the marriage are called into question, and she agonizingly asks herself if she has been wasting her time trying to be a good wife.

In general, the answer is that she hasn't. Marriage guidance counselors take the occurrence of adultery much less seriously than we, or our circle of friends, ever do. For one thing, they deplore the idea of ownership in marriage, and feel that a wife's hurt reaction is often more a feeling of being deprived of a possession. Her complaint that "he doesn't love me any more" is analyzed as being unrealistic, since her husband obviously considers his marriage important when he wants her to remain with him. But she values his exclusive love, and she fears that if he is able to get involved with another woman, there is an area of his personality that she does not know well enough to satisfy.

Yet cases of adultery can often occur without it being in any way her fault. In a period of intensive overwork, a man can be so claimed by office life that a co-worker becomes for a short while the female companion he needs. The overwork will come to an end—and very likely so will his need for the woman. The wise wife, though suffering jealously, may have to realize that at this particular moment, she is not the only prop her husband needs. If she causes scenes and threatens to walk out, she may pull him down just at the moment he needs extra support.

In other circumstances, a woman may be propelled into an outside affair herself. Alice and Bill had been married for ten years, but the last three years of their lives had been clouded by a tragic car accident in which one of their three children was killed. For two years after their son's death, they were sunk in despair together. Their unhappiness was shared, but both of them had forgotten that any other feeling existed. Then, when Alice was advised by her doctor to return to work and take an interest in the outside world once more, she suddenly started an affair with a man in her office.

The wedding ring—symbol of a bond, not bondage. For within the security of an enduring marriage, a man and a woman may explore, as equals, some of the richest experiences that life has to offer.

It was an unrealistic, frivolous relationship; but for the first time in years, she began to realize that a man and a woman could share something more than a heavy burden together. In her naivety, she told her husband. He at first felt the marriage was rocking, but after a while, he realized that what she was saying to him indirectly was: "Happiness is possible. I'm trying it. Can't you try it again? Maybe we could even try together?" In the end, they did make it together.

There are times in many lives when a husband and wife cannot struggle out of a tragedy unaided. What may help them, strange as it may seem, is the intervention of an outsider into their married life.

Many ordinary people are tolerant enough to know this. Some years ago, a national magazine published a letter from a woman reader confessing that, after 11 years of marriage, she felt her whole life was improved by the occasional affair. "I found myself loving my husband more," she wrote. "Perhaps you would call it guilt. I prefer to think it is because he is so wonderful in other ways." The magazine deplored her attitude, and ran a sermon-like article around her letter. Weeks later, it ran a large letters-to-the-editor section containing many letters in support of the woman. The magazine admitted it was wrong in assuming that women would not sympathize with the original writer's point of view. One supporter wrote: "I have been married for 14 years,

and I have a completely happy and compatible marriage. I love my husband in a deeply profound way, but I find that I cannot do without the extra stimulus of a lover to make me feel totally alive. This makes me appreciate my husband more, makes the marriage more interesting and keeps it from falling into a deadly dull routine."

Though these women may be in the minority, they have discovered a truth that is a well-known tradition of marriage in parts of Europe: divorce is less likely if marriage is presumed to be as flexible as life itself, and if adultery is not taken to be an instant sign that the marriage has broken down.

Yet the essence of marriage lies in the exclusive experiences of husband and wife together, not shared by anyone else in the world. An enormous emotional richness exists between two people who have lived together for decade after decade, watched their children be born and grow up, seen the world change around them, and learned to take each other for granted in the best sense of the word. Time and again surveys have been taken to find out what married people value most about marriage. The answer that comes back is the same: companionship and communcation.

The couple that is first brought together by sexuality usually ends with a lifetime dialogue behind them—a long conversation that covers every aspect of living and that only death can end. Marriage begins with physical abandon, with the exploration of each other's bodies by a man and woman. It ends with stability, the sense of safety and trust that makes both partners feel this is real loving, this is real life.

How to Be Your Husband's Mistress

4

For her husband, a woman will make almost any effort. She likes to cook his favorite food, she spends hours selecting fabrics to make their home beautiful, she takes care that the children learn to do things to please him too. Her own delight in living, and her pleasure at pleasing him, she expresses in her appearance and grooming.

But how much time does she spend in thinking about and improving their sexual life together? Frequently she just does not bother at all. After hours spent at a beauty salon, comes the moment when her husband takes her hair down. What happens then? Only too often she has not prepared the next step. It is as though she deliberately prevents herself from considering their sexual lives with the same care she gives to everything else.

The explanation is easy enough to find. As a young girl she was probably brought up and educated to healthy "outgoing" action. She learned to compete with her brain, and strive with her body in games and sports. She was probably advised by her mother to keep her body clean and fresh, and instructed that it must always be free from dirt or disease. What almost certainly was never mentioned to her was that she might also prepare its erotic possibilities. She was never given any idea that the erotic side of a woman should be nurtured and perfected, as any other aspect of living.

Even today, we would be worried by the thought of instructing a child of nine or ten to play with its genitals and learn the pleasure that can bring. It would seem to us like corruption of innocents. Probably we will not change our ideas about this. But

many primitive peoples, and some modern African and Eastern ones, have a tradition of initiating young women into erotic technique. As a result, they start their marriages with some knowledge of how to please and be pleased. The societies also take it for granted that, as wives, the young women will go on learning and acquiring greater art in their lovemaking throughout their married life.

The western woman lacks both preparation and expectations. She often wishes to improve her sexual life, but the wish remains vague and does not lead to any plan of action. Yet it is necessary for the wife to recognize one essential fact above all about her female sexuality. Nature has endowed her with many things, but it has not endowed her with the spontaneous capacity for sexual pleasure that belongs to her husband. It is not possible for a man to complete the sexual act, which ends biologically with the impregnation of the female, without also achieving sexual pleasure. A woman can, and too often in the past has, received the male inside her, and become pregnant as nature intends, without any pleasure at all. For a woman, sexual pleasure is an acquired art. It is little short of tragic that very few young women are made to understand this.

At the same time, it is quite obvious that nature intended women to acquire this art, since it supplied her with an organ that is uniquely equipped for it: the *clitoris*. Though

Monotony is perhaps the greatest single enemy to sexual happiness in marriage. But the woman who recognizes the danger and accepts that variety in lovemaking is not perversion, but healthy and rewarding, is well on the way to defeating marital boredom.

this small organ situated inside the female vulva is frequently described as a tiny penis, this description is not quite correct. The penis in the male has many functions besides that of transmitting sexual pleasure. The clitoris in the female has no other function at all. It exists simply as the focus, the starting point, and transmitter of female sexual pleasure. In learning how to increase her sexual responsiveness, a woman should make the clitoris the center of her thought and attention.

Her husband will thank her for it. Though it is true that pleasure comes more automatically to him, his pleasure is increased by pleasing her. Too frequently, a man who is making love to his wife has a feeling of playing tennis against a wall—the ball comes back automatically, but that is all. He would rather play the game with a real partner who is placing the shots with some thought, care, and skill. If his wife is really enjoying their lovemaking, if her pleasure really matches his own, he will feel more loved and loving, more welcome, and more secure.

Many women might hesitate to follow the advice of the author of *The Sensuous Woman* to undertake a few sessions of masturbation in order to find out how her clitoris responds to stimulation, how she is aroused fastest, and what she likes best. It is, nevertheless, not such bad advice, provided the act leaves no feelings of guilt. After all, many young men first find out about the pleasant sensations of their bodies through masturbation.

Once a woman has worked out what makes her arrive at orgasm surely and pleasurably, she can and must pass the knowledge on to her husband. On the other hand, her relationship with her husband may be such that she is able to ask him to experiment with her, to stimulate her clitoris in different ways, with hand and tongue, roughly or gently, and work out with her by trial and error the place this vital organ of hers has in their lovemaking.

There are other important aspects of her body that she should know, and tell him about. One of the most important is that even after they have worked out techniques to arouse her to her full pitch of sexual excitement, she can lose her path on the road to a satisfying orgasm in even a few seconds if he stops the stimulus. For example, in the few seconds it takes for a man to turn aside and put on a contraceptive, she can fall back rapidly from her plateau of excitement to a much less aroused state. It may be impossible for her ever to get back to the full pitch, so although her husband reaches orgasm unfailingly, she does not. Her nerves are left tingling, her muscles tensed, and her blood vessels swollen for a release that does not come.

The only solution, once they are both aware of this, is to settle for a pattern of stimulation that does not have even a second's interruption. The couple must find a better form of contraception, and the husband must learn to continue stimulating his wife's body until the moment that his penis enters her and takes over the last stage of their pleasure.

But it is not possible to find strict rules of sexual technique that will help every woman to remain the responsive lover that

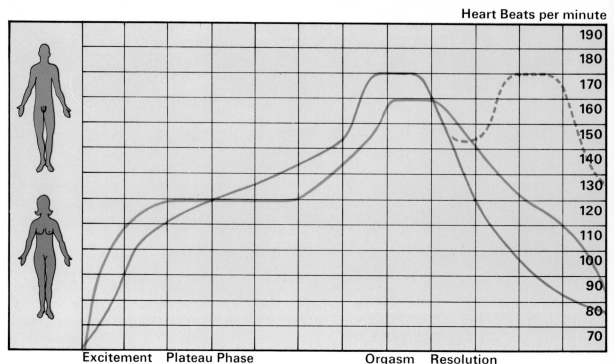

190
180
170
160
150
140
130
120
110
100
90
80
70

Excitement   Plateau Phase   Orgasm   Resolution

This diagram compares the heart rates of a man and a woman during the four phases of sexual response—excitement, plateau, orgasm, and resolution. As the partners enter the excitement phase, the man's heart rate (shown by the blue line) climbs rapidly, but levels out during the plateau phase. It rises again sharply to reach a peak at orgasm, and then gradually slows back to normal. In the woman, heart rate (red line) rises steadily until she reaches her climax, then quickly falls again. Even when a woman goes on to experience another orgasm, her heart rate follows the same pattern (dotted line).

she and her husband want her to be. One of the most important facts about women and their sexuality was discovered by William Masters and Virginia Johnson in the 11 years of study that produced their book *Human Sexual Response*. Though they were able to produce just one chart that shows what leads to orgasm in men, they had to produce several for women. Women are so unalike in their sexual reactions that it is quite difficult to generalize about them. Masters and Johnson talk of "the infinite variety of female sexual responses." Many an old rake has no doubt looked back on the women he has known in life and come to the same conclusion. Every man has to look upon the woman who is his wife as unique

in her sexual reactions. She is unknown territory for him to map, and he should enjoy her individuality.

In every woman, the climax of sex—the orgasm—bestows the same benefits, the same release of tension, the same pleasure, the same emotional leap of unity with her partner as in the male. But after the climax, women differ once again from men. The "afterglow" of intercourse takes longer to fade for women, and they appreciate fondling and kissing *after* intercourse as well as before. This is why they become so upset by a husband who merely rolls over and falls asleep. Sometimes, too, they want more than mere afterglow, for women are capable of multiple orgasm in a way that the male is not. After a lull of a few seconds, many women can continue to a second or third climax without exhaustion. It takes a husband who is a considerate lover to understand this and excite his wife again when his climax is over. Yet the more he understands her body and attends to her needs, the more she will regard him as a lover.

A growing number of women have discovered the delight of the singular female gift for multiple orgasm, although it is an experience that until recently many scientists denied ever existed. When Kinsey first published his studies of *Sexual Behavior in the Human Female* a quarter of a century ago, he included the information that 14 per cent of women he had interviewed had experienced multiple orgasm. This finding was met with surprise by many experts and disbelief by others. Multiple orgasm, they said, was just a fairy tale, and Kinsey had been

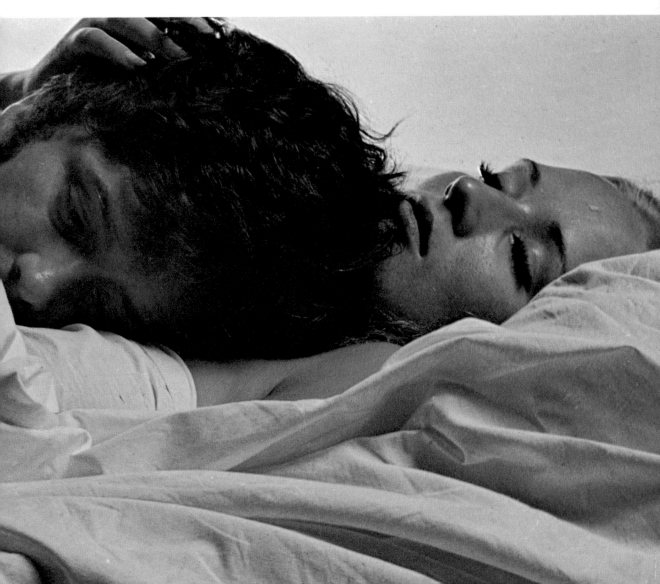

Left: you don't have to look as provocative as this to turn your husband into a Casanova, but using the visual appeal of your body to excite your man can work wonders in enlivening your sex life.

Below: sometimes just a glimpse of a half-undressed wife is enough to arouse a husband's excitement.

taken in. Today, however, there is no argument. Masters and Johnson have observed multiple orgasm in the laboratory. Many women do achieve this, and more could if they and their husbands were aware of it. The secret is for the husband to restimulate his wife almost immediately after her first orgasm, so that her pleasure can go on and on. "Many females," Masters and Johnson insist, "especially when clitorally stimulated, can regularly have five or six full orgasms within a matter of a few minutes." This is undoubtedly the summit of achievement as far as sensual love for women is concerned. Like all mountains, we can begin to learn to climb it once we know that it is there.

As both mistress and wife, a woman must understand and show that she loves every

Right: the sight of his wife undressing can be highly stimulating to a man, and a deliberately tantalizing striptease—whatever you may think of it—can have enormous erotic appeal for your husband.

change and reaction in her husband's body. With understanding she will dare on occasion to take the initiative, to begin their lovemaking by stimulating him, to take command and turn his sexual world upside down. There are few men who do not occasionally long for a woman who will do just that.

It is usually easier in every way to interest a husband in sex. Everything that catches his eye can arouse him. While his wife is not excited by seeing him bend over to change his socks, most men are stimulated by the sight of a half-dressed wife pulling off her stockings. (The modern fashion for tights has been an erotic loss as far as most husbands are concerned). His arousal is easily signaled by the erection of the penis. To many a wife, this direct and truthful reaction of her husband's body to her presence is a source of great delight and amusement.

When she sees that he is aroused, and therefore probably anticipating making love to her, she can sometimes make the first move. She can stroke his shoulders, remove his tie, rub her fingers through the hair on his chest, and show him by touching him how much she loves and notices him. Many women who would not hesitate to pick up and fondle their baby are strangely hesitant in approaching their husbands. It is as though they are behaving according to an etiquette that says they must not speak before they are spoken to, nor kiss before they are kissed. From the most ordinary touch she can move on to more direct sexual invitation. A woman is so used to the idea that a man likes to undress her, that she forgets that he likes to be undressed also.

She has probably learned to kiss expertly by using her tongue and teeth in the early days of their courting, but she should not imagine that because they are now married, such overtures ought to be restricted. Because they legally can have sexual intercourse and need not confine themselves to truncated petting, many men and women, once married, make the mistake of cutting the petting

Above: the ancient Hindus devised numerous erotic techniques for the cultivation of sensual pleasure, including 64 different methods of sexual arousal.

Right: once a woman accepts the fact that sexual pleasure is an acquired art, she and her husband can explore together the countless nuances of erotic delight that their bodies can provide.

short. That makes for a less enjoyable, less significant, and less loving encounter.

Many men are highly sensitive to erotic approaches that are not confined to kisses and the touching of genitals. Among such approaches are the nibbling of his ear, biting of his shoulders, or kneading of his buttocks. Above the base of the spine and at the back of the scrotum are two of the most erotically sensitive points of a man's body. When it comes to handling his penis and testicles, a woman's hands need to be gentlest of all, for this is such a sensitive area that a man may be forced to premature orgasm—or given pain—by harsh handling. Fondling her husband with her mouth or tongue, or wrapping him in her long hair are other possibilities for the sensual wife.

In their love for each other, a man and his wife can play together with a freedom that they have not had since the play of

children. There is very little play about getting dressed up in white to compete at tennis. But there is much play in handling each other while making love. A couple that knows how to frisk about like young animals is as innocent and happy as a couple of young puppies nipping and snapping at each other. Whatever they both want to do in the privacy of their own home is right for them. There is no need to fear that any action that pleases both of them is deviant or harmful.

The idea of being abnormal can be troublesome. It led Jane to her doctor in some anxiety after three years of marriage to ask him about her husband's sexual tastes. Suddenly he had discovered the pleasure of entering her from behind, and this was what he wanted to do each time they made love. "Surely this is 'deviant'?" Jane asked. "It's the way animals couple." Her doctor informed her that, in fact, this position of lovemaking was the most natural thing in the world, but if Jane did not enjoy it, she should tell her husband. There was no *reason* why she should not enjoy it, however, and

couple of drinks can often slow down his responses and help him to extend their lovemaking. Techniques for delaying the husband's climax in order to allow his wife to reach her orgasm at about the same time as he does, have long been the subject of lovemaking manuals of Eastern societies.

A much newer sexual subject is the part orgasm plays in a woman's pleasure. Though most of our modern knowledge of a woman's *need* for orgasm is all to the good, a wife should be aware that it has placed an often unfamiliar burden on her husband—one that can diminish his pleasure if she is not tactful. He can become so anxious about whether she has achieved climax that his anxiety ruins his own pleasure. It would be a very unhappy state of affairs if a woman ever allowed her husband to feel that the competition and stresses of everyday life have entered the bedroom—that she was watching his capacity to give her an orgasm as closely as the boss watches his sales figures. A woman should not fake, but she should learn to be generous. Even if she does not always achieve the pleasure that she anticipates, she should not show strong disappointment nor be accusing. A perpetual failure to achieve orgasm is a problem (see Chapter 7). An occasional failure is just one of life's accidents, and should be treated as such.

What she must never forget is that technique and achievement of pleasure are merely serving love. Even when technique hits a temporary hitch, the love she feels for her husband need not diminish. By keeping their love in proper perspective, she will ensure it for many years ahead. Modern surveys confirm that happily married couples can achieve sexual pleasure together well into their sixties. But this does not depend simply on technique. It depends on desire—and that arises between two people who still love and interest each other.

probably a mental censorship on her part kept her from doing so.

In being the initiator of lovemaking, a woman also discovers the excitement and pleasure of arousing someone else. This will make her understand why her husband experiences excitement in arousing her. When he finally enters her, she can help him to delay his orgasm, and to stretch out their pleasure by alternately resting and moving. If a man ejaculates too soon, it is often as much the fault of the wife as his own. If he has problems in delaying his climax, a

Love and Sex Outside Marriage
5

"Should I or shouldn't I?" is one of the most difficult questions a woman ever has to ask herself. It is a question that does not seem to worry the male sex to the same extent. A man of almost any age accepts the idea more easily that, once he desires a woman, he should go ahead and try to make love to her. It is with the woman that the decision seems to rest, and the question she puts to herself is often put in the most passive way: "Should I let him?" No matter how modern she may think she is, a woman is often disturbed by a feeling that she is giving something away when she agrees to make love to a man who is not yet, or may never be, her husband. She is somehow conscious of man as an aggressor who takes, of woman as a passive creature who gives.

Many maintain that a woman does lose something, and not in the simple physical sense of losing her virginity, with each lover: that she leaves a part of herself with every man she has loved and made love to. Today, however, an increasing number of women question whether this is really so, and instead ask about the possible gains. Even accepting that what most women want, and find most important, is a happy marriage, they wonder if they best ensure that by cutting themselves off from any sexual life outside marriage. Is sexuality a treasure that each woman is born with, something that she must hoard, and keep only for her husband? Or is sex something that, like a muscle, is developed by using it?

How a woman views sexual love depends largely upon her temperament and her upbringing. It may depend partly on her religious ideals, especially if she is of the

Today's sexual climate brings wider freedom —and bigger personal choices. For one woman the only sexual partner must be a husband; for another, any attractive partner could be a lover. The decision is theirs.

Left: for much of the past, when virginity was a girl's passport to marriage, sexual love outside wedlock was harshly condemned. This 18th-century painting shows the desolate loneliness of a girl who defied convention. A letter from her lover has told her he will never return, and she sits holding the watch that is all she has left of him.

Right: these days, no girl has to get married unless she wants to. The single girl can live her life as a free agent, earning her own living, owning her own property, and enjoying her sexuality without committing herself to a lifetime partnership.

Christian faiths that have always emphasized chastity and denial of the flesh. It may depend on her romantic ideas, and ideals of purity and remoteness. Like her bodily reactions to the act of sex itself, her mental and emotional reactions are infinitely varied.

Whatever her own personal attitude is, it will be affected by seeing and accepting what others do—by pressures from society around her. The social climate has changed most of all in the last half century, for very practical reasons. Because women can work and earn their own money, they do not have to think of marriage as the only career open to them. They do not have to worry about virginity as a qualification for entering marriage. They are not, in theory at least, afraid of unwanted pregnancies inside or outside marriage, since modern contraception offers great protection. Modern ideas about the importance of sexuality spur them on, and pressures of conformity are now to have sex rather than to avoid it. Surveys of American college girls have shown that, while 20 per cent were in fact sexually experienced, 75 per cent believed that most of their classmates were.

Today, the girl who makes love for the first time, has a 50 per cent chance of doing so outside marriage. What does it mean to her now to be losing her virginity? It is still, for all women, an event of enormous importance—an end to fantasy and wondering, and a beginning of knowledge and maturity. The circumstances surrounding this first experience make an indelible impression. If it was casual and unpremeditated, it may create a lasting attitude of indifference. If it was uncomfortable and hastily snatched, perhaps in the back seat of a car, it may make a girl think of sexual encounters as uncivilized and brutish. If the young lovers were more fortunate, and were able to make love in peace and privacy, they will have had the chance to talk to each other about their feelings, and to start weaving their sexual contacts into their general pattern of communicating with each other.

"Did we do it right?" a novice may often want to ask, since for her, the first time around, there may have been little pleasure involved, and a lot of anxiety about technique. Where does she go from here? For

Right: are we really as permissive as we think?
The young advocate sexual freedom, but surveys
of college girls—such as these—show that less
than a quarter were sexually experienced. Three-
quarters of these same girls, however, thought
most of their classmates were no longer virgins.

most girls, the bond between her and her lover will be strengthened by their sexual experience together. She will begin to care about him a great deal more in a total way because he will have become a much more significant person to her. The ideal, it may seem to her, even in vague daydreams (and it may seem even more so to her parents), would be that this affair ends in marriage. Sometimes it does. Though both girl and boy may have started out with tentative desire and feeling for each other, both may find that this is not simply an experiment, not a temporary phase, but something much stronger and more continuing that they would like to make permanent. Both may be delighted to find that their first love is also their last love.

However, it may not happen like that. Considering how complex human beings are, it is expecting a great deal that the first partner they choose should be the right one forever. This is one of the arguments used in favor of young people experimenting a little before marriage, in that the partnership can be broken without hard feelings if it does not work out. However, in practice, feelings are liable to be extremely hard. A failed love affair can make someone feel almost as bitter as a failed marriage. Though it may disturb a boy also, it is likely to have a stronger effect on a girl. Women find it hard to recover from what they consider to be a rejection. They are inclined to see the situation from a passive viewpoint and think: "He has rejected me. He was looking for something special in me and I didn't come up to expectations." Frequently, if they could be honest, they would have to

admit that they were also seeking something, they were also trying out their own feelings. Moreover, the experience gave them a chance to learn. They added to their store of emotional and physical knowledge, and they learned more about their own reactions, and something of how a man reacts to love and sex.

Yet many women find it difficult to see the positive side of their experience. Patricia was 19 when she first met Tony. Their attraction to each other started when they were students together. For a long while, they went out together and kissed and petted in Patricia's college room. Then one summer night, when they went swimming together, they finished up making complete love on the beach. Patricia was shattered and pleased at the same time. She began to take Tony more and more seriously, and to make greater efforts to see him and do things for him. After a time, Tony became worried about where they were heading. Patricia was clever in her studies, and he was a little in awe of her. Gradually he found himself increasingly anxious when he was with her. Finally, he was forced to tell her that he did not think they should stay together because her ambitions and her ideas were too demanding, and her possessiveness frightened him. He wanted to end it.

Patricia was shocked and hurt. "How could he do this to me?" she wailed to her friends. At first, she was so depressed that she did badly in class, subconciously trying to prove that she was not too clever for Tony. After a while, she doggedly turned to class work as compensation to prove that she could succeed. It was years later, when she

Below: the opinion of friends can mold a girl's attitude toward sex. If the group favors the free expression of sexual love, she may be pressurized into conforming—or appearing to conform— with this point of view.

On a summer's day, a boy and a girl make love for the first time. For each woman that first sexual experience will have its own unique meaning. For some it will be the start of a lasting relationship. For others, it may be the result of one casual and hurried encounter. However it happens, it may mark a girl's future attitude to sexual love.

was married to a brilliant teacher of equal talents to hers that she was able to see that Tony's instinct had been right.

It is very hard for a young girl ever to realize that love can end, and to accept the fact that love does not always end for two people at the same time.

A wiser, probably older woman will sometimes be able to say, after a relationship has come to an end: "We both went into this with our eyes open. We had some marvelous times together. The memories can never be taken away. I didn't *give* him the best years of my life. He helped to *make* them some of the best years. I have no regrets."

In fact, a failed love affair is easier to recover from than an early marriage that ends in ruin. Many sociologists are warning that the pattern of love and marriage is changing and will settle into a new form. Because of earlier physical maturity, and earlier economic independence, young people expect sex earlier. They will not wait until their middle 20's as many of the older generation did. So society will have to concede either that the young marry early, that they live together unmarried, or that they have considerable premarital experience before making their final choice of a lifetime partner. Many parents today are aware

that their daughters are being pushed toward one or another of these choices. All three alternatives cause worry, especially as statistics show that early marriages often end in divorce.

One successful woman politician, married for the second time, confessed recently: "My daughter is living with a boy she met at college. When they come home to visit, they are quite open about it. I find it difficult to be severe and disapproving, especially when I remember that at her age, I had already made a disastrous first marriage."

What an increasing number of parents are telling their children in advising them how to live healthy sexual lives, is that they must not regard the opposite sex as being there to score points off. They must never seduce and discard other human beings.

This applies to girls as well as boys, though it is boys who are traditionally regarded as liable to be boorish exploiters. They must value themselves highly, and not make love without feeling love. Even more important, they must not produce an unwanted child. Though the facts of contraception can seem alarming and unromantic, young people will be better off to know them and so be able to avoid a tragic unwanted pregnancy.

Given the possibility of real feelings of tenderness in a relationship, and the protection of contraception, there is some evidence that sexual experience before marriage helps a woman adjust to a vital sex life after marriage. The habits of heavy petting, kissing, fondling, and even clitoral stimulation to orgasm, are a help to urgent

adolescents. In addition, Kinsey found that "there is considerable evidence that premarital petting contributes definitely to the effectiveness of sexual relations after marriage."

Kinsey also found in his surveys of the sexual life of women that 77 per cent of those who had complete experience before marriage were able to look back from middle age and see no reason to regret what they had done in their youth. But, predictably,

"premarital coitus that was had with the future spouse was least often regretted." Characteristically, women were seen to give greater value to a youthful passion that has provided the basis for a permanent bond of affection. But even when marriage is not the result of the first partnership, many women feel justified in seeking experience that they feel will be helpful in making their marriage successful.

In some women, experiments lead to

For some young girls, their first love will also be their last. And, despite the much-publicized sexual freedom of the young, many girls today still dream, like their mothers and grandmothers before them, of finding fulfillment through the lasting love and companionship of a happy marriage.

man for her attentions. Inevitably, next day she confessed that she had spent the night with her target man. Though Audrey's behavior puzzled her friends at first, they soon began to sense that she herself was almost as confused about it. Audrey's parents had died in a car crash when she was four years old, and she had been brought up by her grandfather. She had never been quite certain of his love, and had felt a strong insecurity. As an attractive teenager, she found that she suddenly had a powerful weapon in sex—something she could use to gain the attention of others. She used it to the full. However, when she found out what a temporary interest such use of sex gave her, her desperation increased. For in wielding sexuality as a weapon, she never gave love a chance to develop. It was only many years later, when Audrey met an older man who understood her insecurity, and who helped her to know her own feelings and make her body follow those feelings, that she was able to stop her promiscuous wanderings.

The promiscuous drive away what they most crave—love and security. The trap of indiscriminate and casual sex prevents a woman from maturing to the point that she can build a stable, permanent relationship—in or out of marriage. She herself will begin to feel that she is not capable of loving; and many men who encounter her will find it hard to believe that she could ever turn into a loyal wife.

It is a horror of casual sex that makes many people insist that sex should only be enjoyed inside marriage. Yet it is possible in all areas of life to be flexible without

disintegration of character rather than to maturity. These are the women parents and elders have in mind when they issue warnings to the younger generation. They are thinking of some girls who, after their first experience of sex, found it easy to slip into promiscuity.

Audrey enjoyed an erotic reputation as a student for a series of love affairs that she seemed to enter and leave lightly. Her girl-friends would watch with awe at parties as Audrey picked out some attractive young

inviting anarchy. Throughout a long life there may be many occasions—before marriage, after a failed marriage, or during a bout of marital distress—when a woman may want to seek an escape in a love affair. Since the world began, men and women have always done so.

Divorced women find themselves in much the same situation as the adolescent, wanting the affection and physical comfort of men but unwilling to commit themselves to a permanent partnership too soon. In some ways, it is more difficult for a divorcee. Many divorced women admit how hard it is to adjust to a life without regular sex, after having it during marriage. Others are bitter that because many men are aware of a divorcee's difficulties, they treat divorced women as fair and easy game. Some of the clubs for the divorced and separated, though helpful to their members in many ways, also sometimes provide groups of older, disillusioned women who are easy prey to philanderers. For the divorced woman to learn to love and trust again is not easy. Probably she will be wisest to spend some years concentrating on something outside her emotional life, like her work, before beginning to face all the expectations of a new long-term relationship. In the meantime, a love affair that remains just in the emotional shallows may console her and help

A moment's attraction between strangers, a look that says, "Shall we go to bed?"—and a casual affair begins. Perhaps the two will never meet again, or possibly their affair will deepen into a more lasting attachment. While an endless succession of brief encounters may be unsatisfying and even emotionally harmful, there may be moments in a woman's life when a short, intense, and purely sexual affair provides the temporary fulfillment that she needs.

80

her find temporary happiness. She must take care, however, lest its ending prove a painful reminder of the breakup of her marriage.

Not all love affairs, after all, have to be treated with the serious frame of mind that is needed to embark on marriage. Some of the most vivid and enjoyable may be brief encounters. Many of the great lovers of history did not love any one person for long. Most women in middle age can look back on a short, intense experience that they valued. The secret of enjoying an affair fully may well be in a woman's being honest to herself and to the man about what is really expected from the affair. It would not do, of course, to say brutally: "we know this is only for one week"; but it could help to indicate in a subtle way that this is a possibly short-lived fling, without strings attached.

One of the best kept secrets of modern times, with its obsession with youth, is the pleasure of sex in middle age. In the past, the only decent attitude for women after 40 was supposed to be a patient resignation, with a graceful approach to death. Modern surveys confirm that the sexual impulse is still strong in women up to the age of 60, and that it frequently increases after the menopause. Many women find that, in their mature years, they can appreciate and enjoy sex more. They are less obsessed by extravagant ideas

of heroic love than they were in adolescence, and are more ready to understand and value the ordinary human being they are with. They are less tormented by the question of "should I?", and more interested in the delightful details of "how should I?". They may have acquired a more sophisticated ability to take their loving slowly. The young might think them decadent, but they themselves merely feel that they are women who have come to terms with the world. Middle age today often brings with it a sexual fling that asserts that there is life to be lived yet. Our society tends to condemn a middle-aged man or woman who seeks a change from their married partner, but other societies, notably the French, have long recognized that it is possible to love two people—one's own familiar partner, and a new and exciting alternative.

That the rare fling should be subject to such intense disapproval if one or both of the partners is married, may be a misfortune. Adultery is a serious word, and is usually interpreted as a serious blow to a marriage. Yet many individuals have found a necessary escape in a short affair, especially during a stressful period in their marriage. Often it has restored their sense of proportion—and indeed their mental balance—and made them more, not less, able to preserve the marriage that is the real center of their lives. Some marriages seem to require what has been called "an adulterous prop" to keep them going. They may not be very good marriages, but they may be the best that the individuals concerned can create.

Provided that some genuine attempt at a breakthrough in feeling is made in every affair, all the hardships and jealousies that

For the divorced woman, with a broken marriage behind her, the road ahead may seem bleak and empty for a while. She may long for the comfort of male companionship, but fear the involvement of a new relationship that could bring fresh heartbreak.
For her, a temporary affair without emotional committment may offer not just a way out of loneliness, but also the reassurance that she needs to rebuild her shattered confidence in love and life.

The Victorian attitude to adultery was stern and uncompromising. These paintings by Augustus Egg illustrate the downfall of an unfaithful wife. In the first picture, the wife lies sobbing on the floor as her husband shows her his evidence of her infidelity from a letter which he has torn and flung to the ground. The husband sits, grim-faced and hurt, while one of their little daughters leaves off play and turns to look at her parents with fright in her eyes.

Some years have passed. The daughters, as young women, mourn the death of their father. The elder girl gazes out into the moonlight and wonders about her mother's fate.

Under the same moon sits their mother, forced to seek any shelter she can by the riverside. Her thoughts go out to the little girls she left so long ago, as she tries to comfort the illegitimate child she nurses.

they can cause may well be worth bearing. What is quite useless as an escape from a difficult marriage, or in any other circumstances, is mindless partner-swapping such as the pointless exchange of husbands and wives among suburban neighbors, in which no feeling enters except the sense of challenge of a different body. Sex then is merely an alternative to television. Germaine Greer, author of *The Female Eunuch,* warns that constant casting around for new sex partners and new sex methods is a cover up for boredom and that "it does not restore life. Sex in such circumstances is less and less a form of communication and more and more a diversion."

The increasing permissiveness of the modern world has shifted attention away from rigid rules about sexual behavior, and a strong prohibition against sex outside marriage, to more general principles indicating the quality of sexual life that each individual should aim at. In the end, the quality of any woman's sexual life will be determined by her whole personality, which also influences the quality of her intellectual life, her family life, and every other aspect of her existence. To the casual, casual sex will seem all right. To the generous, generous sex will come easily.

All women entering or finishing any love affair will have to recognize two basic facts about human loving. Without some degree of commitment to each other in a love affair, very little is enjoyed or learned by the man or woman. On the other hand, the greater the degree of commitment, the more painful it will be to end the relationship if the less commited partner decides to.

The enjoyment of sexual love does not decrease
with time. Far from it! The years of middle age
and after can be the most delightful of a woman's
sexual life. For this is the time when many a woman
finds that she appreciates and enjoys sex more
than ever. More understanding, more experienced,
and more generous in her loving, the mature woman
may well be better fitted than her younger
sisters to reap the rich rewards of a happy love affair.

Birth Control: The Chance to Choose
6

During the fertile years of an average marriage, a couple will make love about 3,500 times. Though nature did not intend any woman to produce thousands of children, the natural result of marriage for her could be to be pregnant every year until middle age.

This is an intolerable idea to most modern women, but yearly pregnancies was a condition that long prevailed for most women in history. For many centuries, the infant and child mortality rates were so high that families often remained small in spite of a wife's annual childbearing. The large Victorian family of a dozen children was a new phenomenon in the 19th century, because by then medicine had improved enough to ensure the survival of more babies. In this century, we have an entirely new world for women. Today a small family of two children is for the first time the result not of stillbirths and infantile deaths, but of the prevention of annual conception.

This is such an enormous change in the lives of women, that very few authorities or individuals have fully understood what it means. Psychologists who accuse women of envying the male role because they have ambitions outside the home, have not fully absorbed the basic fact that, while 50 years ago a woman could expect to spend one-third of her life in pregnancy and the nursing of infants, today she can expect it to be merely one-fifteenth. Not only does this leave her many years in which to promote other activities, but also it transforms her psychologically (a pregnant woman *is* passive, emotional, womb-centered, and unambitious). It also transforms her marriage.

In the past, when every sexual approach

Today, more and more people have come to realize that families are happiest when new babies are wanted and planned for. Thanks to modern methods of birth control, millions of couples are now having their children by choice—not by chance.

from her husband could mean a further pregnancy for her, even the strongest and most enthusiastic of women must sometimes have dreaded sex. We forget so quickly what that must have been like. It is only too easy to romanticize the past, to look back on the world in which, we think, men were men, and women were women, and family life was like running a small township. It is so easy to forget the horror that frequently lay underneath. In a recent television interview,

the youngest surviving daughter of Leo Tolstoy, the great Russian writer, was interviewed about her life. Immediately the old lady recalled that, being the thirteenth child, she had always been brought up to understand that her mother had spent much of the pregnancy before her birth in jumping off a cupboard, with the desperate hope of having an abortion. If this was what life was like for an upperclass woman at the end of the last century, what was it like for the less privileged peasant woman?

For women now, the undoubted blessings of modern birth control have meant that marriage today does not have to be like that. Though reliable contraception also protects the unmarried and the adulterous, and should prevent the unhappiness caused by so many "shotgun" weddings, its most important role is almost certainly in allowing a husband and wife, who regularly make love to each other, to plan if and when they intend to have another child. In such a

Right: in the past. a pregnancy a year from marriage to middle age was the lot of most wives, such as the mother of 20 children shown here. The ever-present fear of an additional pregnancy, and the exhausting round of childbearing and child rearing, took its toll of a woman's health and sexual happiness, and gave her little chance of any achievement apart from motherhood.

modern marriage, the wife gains in every way. She can delight in her own and her husband's sexuality, and she can enjoy the children she does have without being overburdened.

This is not to say that modern birth control is always easy to work out, but only that it is easier than before. Today there is a wide choice of contraceptive methods available to men and women, but probably none of them are totally trouble-free. As soon as she is married, and probably before, any modern woman should find out all that she can about the different methods, and begin to think about what best fits the life of herself and her husband. It is not a romantic subject. It is not research that any young bride-to-be will look forward to. But it is one of the practical bases for the happiness of her married life. As such, it should come high on her list of essentials. In her mother's generation, most couples postponed getting advice about birth control until *after* they

had produced the two or three children they wanted. Today, many couples like to plan to have several years to themselves before the children arrive, and they seek contraceptive advice from the start.

They'll first learn that the most discussed contraceptive—one that does not involve the couple in doing anything at the peak of the excitement and abandon of the sex act—is the justly famous Pill. This oral contraceptive has now been around for over a decade. Something like a million American women regularly take it. Consisting of massive doses of the natural sex hormones, estrogen and progesterone, the contraceptive pill suppresses the monthly release of the egg, so that invading sperm entering the uterus find no egg to fertilize. It was discovered by Professor John Rock and Dr. Gregory Pincus after they had been treating women patients with estrogen-progesterone doses to regulate their periods.

In using the pill, a woman takes one every

day for 21 days. She then stops the daily dosage for a few days, during which her period will start. Several days later, she resumes taking a pill daily.

It sounds like the easiest, least embarrassing thing on earth. And because it is so close to 100 per cent effective as a contraceptive, it has been hailed as a great step forward. For the majority of women who use it, it certainly is. However, nothing is perfect in this world, and the pill is not perfect for everyone. It does have certain physical and emotional consequences for some women that can make them ill or miserable, and in such cases, they may need to seek other contraceptive methods. There are many varieties of the Pill, and in theory, there is one to suit every woman. But many women feel that, after a couple of experiments (and each period of experiment will have to last about three months to allow her system to settle down to the hormones), they do not wish to go on with trials that produce sickness and overweight, loss of sexual desire, some bleeding, or—very rarely—thrombosis. On the other hand, as advocates of the Pill

point out, none of the side effects of the Pill, felt by a minority of women, are nearly as dangerous as the side effects of pregnancy. In the majority of women, moreover, the Pill can produce a feeling of physical well-being and mental relaxation.

Some experts wonder if the physical side effects of the Pill are, in reality, its psychological side effects. The basic fact about the Pill is that, if taken according to instructions, it will prevent pregnancy. Many women dislike anything so definite. Though they do not want the conception of their children to be totally unplanned, neither do they want the guaranteed sterility of the Pill. They would like to feel that there may be a chance of getting pregnant; that their husband's love still has the power of creating a new life in them. For such women, a slightly less reliable system of birth control may be a benefit. It *may* be as effective as the Pill, but it may not, and this will make them prefer it.

What, then, are the other birth control methods that a woman can turn to?

For a wife who wants the reassuring feeling that she is in charge of the contraceptive side of her sexual life, but does not want to take the Pill, the next most popular method of birth control is the diaphragm. Like the Pill, this device comes in many and various forms that are designed to suit a wide range of variations in female anatomy, and again, it should be obtained from a doctor or clinic.

Above: the development of reliable contraception has helped to transform modern marriage into an equal sexual partnership. Today, for the first time in history, women have the chance to look forward to the pleasure of lovemaking without fear of bad consequences, and a husband and wife can decide for themselves if and when they will have a child.

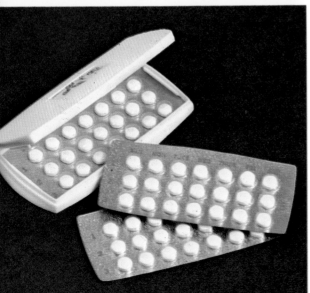

Left: the contraceptive pill—the most effective method of birth control available. A wide variety of brands come in packs like these, designed to make it easy for a woman to check whether she has taken a pill on any particular day. About 20 million women all over the world now use the pill, but it is not necessarily the ideal contraceptive for everyone.

91

Diaphragms are small rubber devices that are inserted in the vagina before the sex act, and because they may be inserted several hours before, there is no last-minute interruption in lovemaking.

They shut off the entrance of the uterus so that no sperm can get into it to fertilize the egg. For greater efficiency, diaphragms are first smeared with jellies or creams that kill male sperm. These creams are usually effective for about three hours. If the sex act does not take place until past the three hours, fresh cream should be applied. The diaphragm cannot be felt inside a woman's body either by her or her husband during lovemaking, no matter how athletic.

This system is highly effective, though not as near perfect as the Pill. Pregnancy can accidentally occur if the diaphragm fits badly—perhaps because a woman did not return to her doctor for checkups—or if spermicidal jellies are not properly applied. There have also been other, more mysterious, occasions when the diaphragm has not worked. Research undertaken in the laboratory by the leading team of William Johnson and Virginia Masters established one new fact that takes away some of the mystery. If a husband and wife make love in a variety of positions, there is a danger that, each time

the penis is withdrawn and reinserted, it can shift the diaphragm. Once the wife is sexually excited, her own internal dimensions change. The withdrawal and reinsertion of her husband's penis at this stage can dislodge the diaphragm. However, if this is kept in mind, the diaphragm is still an efficient modern means of contraception.

The diaphragm, of course, does not suit everybody. Some women are unexpectedly prudish about inserting any object into their own bodies, although sanitary tampons have made them more used to the idea. Others are just plain forgetful. Judy and her husband were invited away for a weekend by some friends who lived in the country. They managed to arrange for grandparents to take care of their two daughters, so that they could have a much needed break together. Before she set off, Judy tossed the small plastic box containing her diaphragm into her makeup case. They arrived at their friends' house, spent a relaxing afternoon swimming at a nearby beach, and that evening enjoyed a marvelous dinner, including wine and liqueur. By the time they went to bed, both Judy and her husband were feeling amiable and amorous. Imagine Judy's consternation when she found that the plastic box that should have contained

In a world where at least three babies are born every second and problems of overpopulation become more pressing, many governments and voluntary organizations are increasingly promoting family planning.

Left: this poster from India stresses the economic benefits of a smaller family. On the left, a family of seven children trudges along, downcast and miserable. But the family on the right, with only three children, has been able to buy a car and drive out to enjoy themselves on a picnic.

Right: a British poster makes a more emotional appeal by trying to show a man what it might be like if he were the one to bear the burden of an unwanted pregnancy.

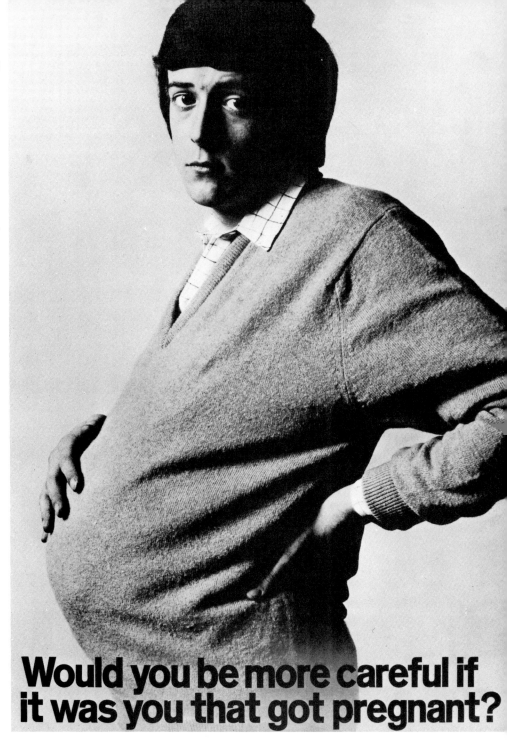

Would you be more careful if it was you that got pregnant?

her diaphragm was empty. She then remembered that she had not put it away in its usual place, but had left it wrapped in a tissue in the bathroom cabinet at home. Neither Judy or her husband were in any mood to be deterred by the lack of the diaphragm. Next year they were gazing ruefully at their third daughter.

A diaphragm is a thing, and like all things, it can be forgotten, lost, or mislaid at just the wrong moment. Women keep their diaphragms in the most unexpected places, such as in cosmetic jars in the bathroom, or in spice jars in the kitchen. It does not matter where they keep the contraceptives as long as they remember to insert them for *every* time they have sex. Then they will not get pregnant. It is more often than not their

memory, rather than the diaphragm, that fails them.

There is a third widely used contraceptive method for women. This is the IUD, or intra-uterine device. The IUD is a plastic loop or coil that is inserted into a woman's uterus by a doctor. In some way that doctors do not yet fully understand, this coil renders the uterus hostile to the implanting of the female egg. The IUD usually remains in place indefinitely. Because it does not require remembering to follow directions, or keeping . track of dates, the IUD is highly recommended for use in the underdeveloped countries, in which women have little chance to become literate.

The IUD is not recommended for women who have never had children, since the cervical canal into the uterus is generally not wide enough to allow the coil to be inserted, and surgical stretching would be needed. Pregnancy cannot occur while the IUD is in position. However, there can be troublesome side effects, such as intermittent bleeding, heavy periods, abdominal pain, and in some rare cases, infection. Also, some women automatically reject the IUD from their uterus and it escapes without their knowledge. Because of these disadvantages, the IUD has less appeal than the diaphragm or Pill.

None of the chemical or mechanical ways of interfering with the process of conception are accepted by the Roman Catholic Church. Any doting husband and wife who know that their last child was an "accident", and

that it was only the inefficiency of their birth control method that brought the baby into the world, get a glimpse of the terrifying human problem that is at the center of the whole subject of contraception. This problem is regarded more as a religious than a human question by the Vatican, which has concluded that no one but God can decide who lives and who dies. No method of controlling who gets born is acceptable to the Catholic Church except that of abstaining from sex. Self-denial as a means of birth control is called the rhythm method. In practicing it, husband and wife who wish to avoid further pregnancy only make love to each other during the infertile, or "safe", period of the month.

What is the "safe period", and how safe is it? The average woman has a 28-day menstrual cycle, and midway between her periods she ovulates—that is, she produces the egg that, if fertilized by her husband, will develop into a baby. Her day of ovulation can sometimes be traced by taking her temperature each morning immediately after waking for one month. At a certain point in the month (which is, at the same time, the middle of the period), there is a noticeable rise in temperature. This is the day of ovulation. If she and her husband want a baby, and they make love in the next three or four days after ovulation, there is a good chance she will get pregnant. If they deliberately stop making love for those same few days, there is a good chance she will not get pregnant. Thus Nature, says the Church, has provided her own clue to family planning.

Unfortunately, it is only a clue. Women vary so much in their menstrual cycle that the ovulation period cannot be precisely pinned down. Many women do not have exactly the same cycle each month. Therefore the rhythm method, which depends on tracing each individual woman's own rhythm with total accuracy, is difficult to put into practice. The cycle can be thrown off by illness, emotional upsets, travel, and other factors. After childbirth, and for some years during menopause, a woman's periods may stop and start in an irregular way. Pinpointing ovulation then becomes almost impossible. Ovulation can also occur spontaneously, as a result of intense orgasm. Many women believe the total fallacy that they cannot conceive while they are breastfeeding, and grow careless about whichever contraception method they are using. They then frequently conceive immediately after the birth of one child, and are burdened with two infants that are referred to as "twins a year apart."

Aside from the ineffectiveness of the rhythm method of birth control, it is considered unacceptable to many because it so frequently denies spontaneous sex. Also it may limit sexual love to those days of a woman's cycle when she may be feeling less

95

responsive, for many women feel more interested in sex just after ovulation, when they are the most fertile. To many who follow the rhythm method, the kitchen calendar can become a symbol of the arid and anxious discipline of their sexual lives.

Many men and women, of whatever religion, have been using mechanical methods of contraception for centuries.

The classic male contraceptive—the condom, or sheath—has been in use since the 18th century, when it was primarily valued as a preventative against infection. Today millions of men still buy these light rubber covers for the penis without any complications, such as the need of a doctor's prescription. They are effective contraceptives provided that they are used in time, every time, and are also removed promptly. It is important that the husband puts the condom on as soon as he achieves an erection and withdraws the protected penis as soon as possible after orgasm, so that the condom does not slip off.

Above: before deciding which contraceptive method to use, a woman should visit her doctor or a birth control clinic to get the skilled advice of someone who is trained to discuss the emotional, as well as the physical, considerations of her particular case.

Right: this chart gives you the most important facts about the chief methods of birth control. The efficiency of each method depends not only on the contraceptive or technique itself, but also on whether it is used regularly and correctly. For this reason, effectiveness cannot be measured with total accuracy. However, the approximate rates of efficiency listed here can be a useful guideline.

The Methods

	What is it?
Pill	Pills containing synthetic trogen and progesterone mones.
Coil or Loop Intrauterine devices (IUD)	Small flexible devices different sizes and sha inserted into the uterus.
Diaphragm (together with spermicidal cream or jelly)	Soft rubber cap with fle metal rim that fits entrance to the uterus.
Condom	Thin, strong rubber cove fitted over the penis.
Spermicidal agents (1) Jellies, creams, soluble tablets, vaginal suppositories.	Chemicals put into vagina.
(2) Aerosol vaginal foam.	Foaming cream in aer can.
Rhythm method ("safe period")	Finding out time of ovula by keeping record of pe dates and temperat changes.
Douche	Syringe filled with wate other special solution.
Withdrawal (coitus interruptus)	
Sterilization	Surgical operation.

Condoms have great disadvantages from the point of view of sexual enjoyment. First, they are a barrier, no matter how thin they might be, between husband and wife, and prevent much of the "feel" of the penis in the vagina; secondly, the contraceptive must be applied at a bad moment in love-making, just before the erected penis is to be inserted. The need to withdraw the penis immediately after orgasm also cuts short any possibility of sexual afterplay. From the standpoint of sheer pleasure for husband and wife, these are serious and inhibiting factors —even if not nearly as inhibiting as the fear of making the wife pregnant.

There are a number of other methods, but most combine the disadvantages of a high accident rate with other aesthetic displeasure. Aerosol foams for women deposit antisperm chemicals in the vagina, but the foam does not always reach far enough down the vaginal passage to provide total protection. Ointments and jellies, used on their own, are similarly hit-or-miss in their efficiency.

How it works	Advantages	Disadvantages	Effectiveness
Taken daily for a certain number of days each month, prevents release of egg.	Easy to use. No interference with enjoyment.	May cause unpleasant side effects. Prescription required.	0.5% pregnancy rate.
Prevents fertilized egg from implanting in uterine wall.	Usually stays in place indefinately. Cannot be felt. Does not reduce pleasure.	Temporary discomfort after insertion. May be expelled without knowing it.	With newest types of IUD 1% pregnancy rate.
Used in conjunction with cream or jelly, prevents sperm from entering the uterus.	No side effects. Cannot be felt by either partner. Can be inserted up to three hours before intercourse.	Must also use cream or jelly. Should not be removed for at least six hours after intercourse.	With correct fit and good cream, 95-98% effective.
Prevents sperm from reaching the uterus.	Easy to obtain. Simple to use.	Can be felt. May slip off. Must be put on at time that interferes with enjoyment.	5-6% pregnancy rate. If woman uses spermicidal cream or jelly less than 5% pregnancy rate.
Immobilizes or kills sperm.	No prescription needed. Usually easy to obtain.	Must be applied again before each intercourse. May cause irritation.	Not reliable unless used with diaphragm or condom.
Forms a chemical barrier against sperm.	No prescription needed. More effective than creams or jellies when used on its own.	Must be inserted again before each intercourse. May cause irritation.	At worst, 20% pregnancy rate. At best, 90-98% effective.
Intercourse is limited to woman's infertile period, just before and just after ovulation.	No pills or devices involved. Only method approved by Roman Catholic Church.	Keeping careful records required. Limits intercourse. Not reliable if periods are irregular.	About 20% pregnancy rate.
Washes out vagina to remove semen before it enters the uterus.	None.	Must be done *immediately* after intercourse. Unreliable. May cause infection.	Least effective of all methods.
Man withdraws penis before ejaculation.	No product required. No cost.	Interferes with sexual climax. Unreliable.	Poor.
In a man, prevents sperm from being released in seminal fluid. In a woman, blocks the passage of eggs from the ovaries to the uterus.	Almost always permanently effective. No need for any other birth control method. Does not interfere with sexual desire or enjoyment.	Cannot be undone.	Virtually 100%.

Inefficient and destructive of pleasure is the method of having the husband withdraw the penis before ejaculation, though it is probably the most ancient and widely practiced birth control method of all. It means that the husband has his orgasm outside his wife's body, and frequently results in accidental pregnancies because some seminal fluid may leak out before the orgasm. It also spoils a lot of sensual pleasure. The husband is isolated at the moment that he should be most conscious of being joined to his wife. It is almost impossible for the wife to achieve her orgasm in the absence of the penis. Still further, it creates a state of anxiety, for both partners worry whether or not the husband will stop his spontaneous lovemaking just before the climax. For any woman who truly wants to achieve sensual pleasure with her husband, withdrawal before ejaculation should be abandoned.

There is an entirely different birth control method that is currently gaining more recognition because of its total efficiency: it is sterilization—both for men and women. Today, a sterilization operation for a woman is still a major one, necessitating the cutting and tying of the fallopian tubes, so that the egg cannot travel to the uterus. Most doctors will not even consider it for their younger patients unless it is an emergency situation in which the wife would almost certainly die of a further pregnancy. However, a number of older women do have a hysterectomy for the removal of the womb some time before the menopause, on their doctor's advice. This is also a sterilization operation, but it is rarely done for reasons of birth control, even though it does have the end result of freeing a middle-aged woman from the fear of an unwanted final pregnancy.

Within the last two or three years, sterilization for men has suddenly become not only an interesting proposition in theory, but also one that a number of couples are seeking in practice. It is estimated that over one

Below: how a sterilization operation works. In a man (left), a piece of each of the *vas deferens* (sperm-carrying tube) is removed, and the cut ends are tied off to prevent them rejoining. In a woman (right), an inch is cut from each Fallopian tube, the duct that carries the egg from the ovary to the uterus. The cut ends are then bent back and tied.

Right: sterilization does not affect health or sexual desire. But it is almost always irreversible, and should only be decided on after long and careful consideration by both partners. However, when a husband and wife are certain that they do not want to have any more children, they may agree that this is the best method of contraception for them.

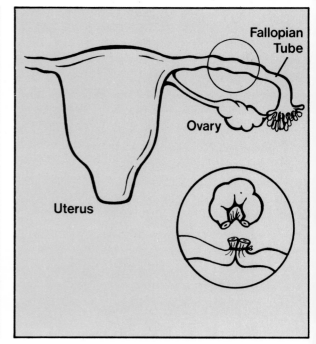

million men in the United States had this operation in 1971 alone. The male sterilization operation, called vasectomy, is extremely simple. It consists of tying or cutting the sperm-carrying tube, and it takes only minutes to perform. It is painless, and it is not expensive.

Sterilization raises serious questions from many points of view. First of all, it is permanent, if the spermatic tube has been cut. There is no chance of restoring fertility. Even if the tube was only tied, doctors have been able to untie it and restore fertility in only a few cases. There is no certainty of being able to reverse the operation. So any man who plans to have a vasectomy should clearly regard it as a permanent step. Should a sterilized husband or wife later enter on a second marriage, they will have

no chance of altering their earlier decision in order to have children with their new partner. To a young man or woman still in their 20's, this many not seem a very relevant argument—especially if they already have all the children they want. But if at the age of 35 they find themselves with a new partner, it could be of vital importance.

Secondly, no one really knows how a man or woman is going to react emotionally to being rendered sterile. Many women feel deeply depressed after an operation removing the womb, even when it was necessitated by the threat of serious disease. They are strongly aware that any hope of motherhood is over, years before nature intended that they become infertile.

What about men? Does a vasectomy adversely affect their pride in carrying on

Left: this 19th-century painting illustrates the traditional fate of the unmarried mother. Despite the pleading of her younger sister, she and her baby are banished from the family home and cast out into the street to survive as best they can.

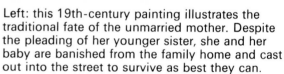

Right: a single girl—or a wife—who is faced with an unplanned pregnancy may decide to seek an abortion. The decision is a hard one, no matter what the circumstances, and the ending of her pregnancy may leave a woman with feelings of guilt and depression.

the family name? The Association for Voluntary Sterilization in the United States quotes a letter from a man of 69, who had the operation in 1938, and who had only good to say of it. "My sexual enjoyment and that of my partner has been enhanced from that day on by the complete lack of fear of unwanted pregnancies, and the absence of having to concern ourselves with precautions of any kind. As to virility, I can ski as well as ever after 45 years of enjoying it, and in summer paddle my kyak down the wildest rivers. How ridiculous it is to prolong the myth that a man's virility depends on his ability to procreate children."

Of course, there is no physical deterioration after sterilization, no loss of sexual desire or skill in the sterilized male. But some men who can no longer father a child certainly feel a sense of loss. Though many birth control experts, impressed by the simplicity of male sterilization, dismiss such ideas as sentimental nonsense, vasectomy is obviously a very important step for many men, and one that needs to be thought out

well beforehand. There is some evidence that in "problem families," a vasectomy can become one more problem. It takes a very self-assured male not to feel threatened by genital surgery, no matter how simple.

The most desperate—and, unless medically supervised, the most dangerous—of all forms of birth control is abortion. Though abortion was, in the past, the only way that a woman could free herself of an unwanted pregnancy, there are so many other methods today that abortion should only be sought as a last resort. In countries where abortion is now legal and relatively easy to get, such as Great Britain, experts are saying that even

with qualified medical attention, there can be some physical dangers for the women concerned (though not the accidental sterility that was so often the tragic result of "back street" abortions). The psychological problems that remain for a woman who has taken the step of rejecting a fetus within her, can be much worse than the physical side, but this depends largely on a woman's personality.

When Anne discovered that she was pregnant, she thought of it as nothing short of disaster. She was in her final year of medical school, training to be a doctor. Her boyfriend was simply that and no more —a student friend with ambitious plans for his career in which immediate marriage and a family did not figure. What could she do? Anne decided she must get an abortion. She knew only one person who was willing and able to perform an operation in their country, and she went to him. After the abortion, Anne felt physically well, studied hard, and completed her examinations satisfactorily. Soon after, she met and fell in love with a man she decided to marry. Her consternation when she came to make love to her new husband was extreme. She found that she had become completely frigid. She simply could not bear sex. On seeking a doctor's advice, she was told that this was something that had happened a number of times before to other women who had had abortions in similar circumstances. The guilt that she had felt about her abortion had set up a self-punishing attitude. As a result, she was refusing to allow herself to relax and feel any pleasure. She gradually overcame her problem with expert help.

The emotional reactions to abortion can be widely varied. Doctors have long been amazed at cases of single girls who have arranged adoptions for their illegitimate babies, with apparent calm, only to arrive back at the office next year, pregnant again, and this time determined to keep the child. Women who have abortions often suffer a similar sense of child loss, and they too set about getting pregnant again. "Women seem driven to get themselves pregnant,"

one leading gynacologist said, in discussing this particular situation.

Indeed they are. It seems to be part of the basic sex instinct in many women to want to be pregnant, and produce children. If their husbands at no point give them the go-ahead to satisfy their instinct, they will often become disturbed and antisocial—and choose the most inappropriate moment of all to assert themselves. To a happily married women with two or three children, family planning often means planning to have no more children. But for some young married women, modern birth control can pose a problem. Its efficiency can allow their husbands to postpone for years, and perhaps forever, the arrival of children. But for most women, the climax of the sex act comes with the birth of her child, and not simply with the orgasm. Birth control for her must be the right to plan having a family as well as not having one.

Today, there is no need for a couple to have a family if they do not wish to. But most women have a deeply felt need to bear and rear at least one child. For them, the greatest benefit of modern birth control lies not in postponing the birth of children indefinitely, but in having the babies they want when they want them and can enjoy them to the full.

When Sex Goes Wrong

7

Everything seems ready today for the full flowering of sensual love for women. Women are encouraged, as never before, to think that sexual pleasure is healthy and desirable. They marry with ideals of love and companionship far higher than previous generations. They are relieved of the burdens of perpetual pregnancy by modern birth control, and are initiated into childbirth without fear when they do want children.

Women are encouraged to be mentally alert and responsive, and not live their lives bored with their traditional place in the home. They are offered cosmetics and clothes that only a princess in ancient civilizations could ever have dreamed of. All is prepared for them to be lively, and sexy—provided, of course, that they actually feel like it.

None of these favorable circumstances

Sex is too vital and complex not to raise problems, but many of them may be temporary. For example, if a family is having emotional or financial difficulties, a woman may find herself unwilling or unable to respond to her husband's sexual approaches.

that surround her modern life is any use to her at all if she doesn't have the feeling for it. In fact, knowing that everything is provided for her, and only her lack of feeling prevents her from living a life that is sexually satisfying increases her anxiety and guilt. In the past, society expected a woman to be chaste and abstain from sex for much of the time, to submit herself to the lovemaking of her husband so that he could satisfy himself and she could bear children. If she didn't enjoy it, so much the better. This fact was a cast-iron guarantee of her refinement. Today the expectation is all the other way. She is bombarded by movies and magazines, advertisements and books that preach or slyly suggest sexual pleasure. Everyone, she is made to feel, is having a good time, is having a full sex life, except her. She alone is just plain frigid.

It is unlikely that anyone can achieve perfection in sex, any more than in other aspects of living. Women are human beings, not goddesses. Like all human beings, they can sometimes display qualities and attractions and talents that no one would have dreamed of. At other times, they can be a sad disappointment to themselves and others. It has long been a legend that a really beautiful woman, as opposed to a merely pretty woman, is one whose looks change constantly from day to day, from moments of marvelous good looks to moments of comparative plainness. Perhaps it is true that a really loving woman is also like that: a kaleidoscope of constantly mobile feelings, whose colors and patterns are not totally predictable, and who can delight but also disappoint.

It would be a rare woman indeed, who in the course of a long life, never went through a phase in which she temporarily lost interest in sex, got bored with her husband, found life generally lacking in excitement, or felt full of problems rather than pleasure. Life is long, and is full of downs as well as ups. Marriage and love are also long-term experiences. They never stay the same. Marriage is bound to have its good years and bad years, like any other creative process. Sex, which lies at the heart of marriage, is bound to be involved in the good and bad.

The greatest problem is a feeling in either partner that they either can't make love, or that if they do, it won't be any fun. Excitement becomes something that they remember with nostalgia, but that they no longer experience. Pleasure, instead of being a spontaneous and healthy reaction, becomes a much talked-about sensation that they feel they have to learn. Like a person who loses the natural appetite for food, like a man or woman who loses the ordinary capacity to sleep, a husband or wife who loses the desire for physical love is demonstrating clearly that all is not well. They may indeed be physically below par, for nothing destroys bodily pleasure sooner than illness or disease. A man or woman with anything as minor as a cold will find it just that much more difficult to feel comfortable, let alone responsive or excited; and mental ill health is an even greater killer of pleasure. A bout of depression, which is one of the commonest of all illnesses, can reduce the world to grayness, and deaden a man or woman's responses. It is a rare individual who never encounters such a bad patch in life. When it comes, for whatever reason, the individual's entire capacity for living is reduced, and with it his or her capacity for a healthy sex life.

The circumstances that result in periods of

to function sexually. They may become totally impotent, and fail to achieve or maintain an erection when they approach their wives; or they may suffer from a more minor malfunction, such as ejaculating too soon. Whatever the difficulty, the best cure is in the tolerant understanding of their wives. If the problem continues for a long period, a man may need to see a doctor or psychiatrist. In most cases, if a wife patiently stands by her husband as he tries to overcome whatever the central problems of his life are, she will help him back to balance and confidence—and eventually to renewed sexual pleasure.

Many times, a man's temporary halt in sexual performance does not reach a serious state, but is just a fleeting reaction to day-to-day pressures. Sheer overwork, a heavy attack of flu, an anxiety about money—these things can get on top of any man, and reduce his interest in sex. The essential point is not to allow a minor failing to build up into a major problem. If his wife can be relaxed and reassuring about it, a husband will treat the whole mishap as incidental.

Similarly, when a woman is afflicted with a temporary loss of interest in sex, her husband must show patience and understanding. If she has usually enjoyed her sex life, she and her husband should not worry too much about the situation. It may be easy to see that she is suffering from overwork and exhaustion, too much worry about her children or her job, or anxieties about their economic condition.

Whenever there is a conflict between husband and wife, that conflict can show up in their sexual lives. A man and woman

sexual malfunction are mysterious and difficult to chart. One of the best known modern writers, Ernest Hemingway, was remarkably frank about his various periods of impotence, and the strain that this problem imposed on his wives. Not everyone is as self-revealing as Hemingway, but numerous men hit periods of self-doubt in which they lose their self-confidence, or are afraid of being dominated by their wives. During such times, they may unconsciously express their fears and anxieties in the most direct way of all: they cease

Right: exaggerated myths of sexual prowess may make a man feel anxious about his own skills. The legendary exploits of Don Juan (shown in a 19th-century print) are a prime example of tales of incredible sexual capacity and expertise. But Don Juan was a fictitious character, and no one alive can hope to achieve sexual happiness by striving after superhuman performance.

can find it difficult to make love when they feel confused or irritated. On many occasions, minor tussles can be soothed away by a session of enjoyable lovemaking. It is no use for a woman to go to her doctor and complain that her sex life has dwindled to nothing, and that she is afraid she is frigid, when the simple fact is that, for the moment, she hates or fears her husband. Sex is a line of communication, and like someone using a telephone, one of the partners can abruptly hang up or slam down the receiver to cut off that communication when they are overwhelmed by negative feelings.

Women can go off sex for the oddest reasons. But once the reason, however odd, has come to light, and been talked about by husband and wife—and perhaps with a doctor—the problem can often be resolved quickly. Jane and Peter had looked forward to their first baby with great pleasure, and were delighted when a daughter was born. For a while after the birth, it was accepted by both of them that Jane, who had had

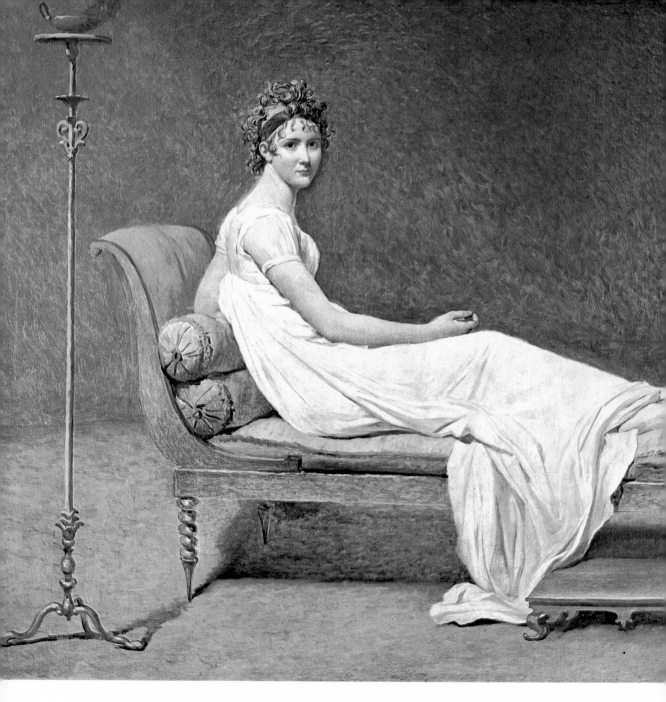

some stitches after her difficult labor, would not feel well enough to make love. Their doctor had told them that many women, for a variety of reasons, ranging from needing time to heal to feeling overwhelmed by the new chores of baby care, are not ready for sex again for a few weeks. But Jane's problem turned out to be more serious. Even by the time her baby daughter was six months old, she was still resisting all efforts on her husband's part to make love to her. She finally realized that something was wrong.

When she went to her sympathetic family doctor to talk over what birth control methods she ought to use in the future, she hesitantly mentioned that her sex interest had not returned again after the birth of her baby. Her doctor wisely showed no surprise, but got Jane to talk about what her present feelings were about sex. It turned out that Jane, who had always enjoyed making love to her husband as a carefree young married woman, was now suddenly burdened by an almost unconscious feeling that "mothers

Left: Madame Récamier, a famous beauty of the 18th century, was known for seductive charm. She combined a delightful sensuousness with a grace and modesty that made men her slaves. But most wooed her in vain. For Juliette Récamier is said to have been frigid, and to have remained a virgin until she was 41 years old.

Right: many women who go through temporary sexual difficulties may develop a fear of being frigid. That fear then can breed new tensions, making sexual pleasure even harder to attain. Whatever the emotional reasons behind inability to enjoy sex, the first step toward solving the problem is to try to overcome the worry that sexual pleasure will never come along again.

don't". Somewhere at the back of her mind, she had the feeling that, along with the responsibility of motherhood, came a more serious attitude to life in general, and that sex was a bit too undignified to have a part in this. She also felt that she was now much more like her own mother—and suspected that her mother had never approved of sex even inside marriage. After her doctor had talked to her like a kindly parent—and very subtly "gave her permission" to be both a mother and lover—Jane solved her conflict.

The problem of frigidity is one on which there is no agreement among the experts. It is surrounded with confusion. In the first place, there is no agreement about what the word means. Does frigidity mean a condition in which a woman feels no sexual excitement or pleasure, and would be content to go through life without any sexual encounter at all? If it means this, it is a very rare condition indeed, touching a tiny percentage of women. Does frigidity mean a condition in which a woman finds

it hard to achieve a simultaneous vaginal orgasm every time she makes love with her husband? If this is the definition, then something like 75 per cent of women are frigid. This is obviously ridiculous, and means that sexual normality for women is being defined in such exacting or unreal terms that the majority of normal women cannot achieve it.

While the experts argue, however, most ordinary people are aware of what they themselves mean by a frigid woman. To them, a frigid woman is either one who has never begun to enjoy her sexual life; one who for some reason has temporarily lost the ability to enjoy it; or one who, too soon in life, has allowed herself to think that she and her husband are now too old for that sort of thing.

Frigidity is something that all women fear. The word alone arouses great anxiety, and anxiety only increases all sexual problems.

Before any woman can enjoy her sex life, she has to conquer anxiety, brush from her mind the worry that things will go wrong, and concentrate on the simple, relaxed responses of her skin, her muscles, her body.

The only point on which all experts appear to agree is that the inability to enjoy sex is always a problem that has its origin in the mind, and not in the body. There are occasional cases of women having physical defects that make sex painful or difficult, but such physical abnormalities are extremely rare. What makes sex painful to some women is their painful attitude to it.

Some of these attitudes are so severe, and so deeply rooted, that a marriage can go for months, even years, without being consummated. The problem only comes to light when the wife approaches a doctor or a birth control clinic with the pretended intention of finding out about birth control, but with the equal hope of finding out why

Right: the frictions of a relationship that has become unsatisfying may all too easily flare up into a hostile battle between husband and wife.

Below: a satirical "before and after" view of marriage. In the first engraving, the woman charms her suitor with sweet harmonies on the harp. In the second, the wife's frantic paino-playing drives her husband to exasperation, and he retreats behind his newspaper. The baby howls in the nursemaid's arms, and even the two lovebirds in their cage have turned their backs on each other.

she resists sex altogether. In such situations, the wife's difficulties usually have the effect of upsetting the husband so much that he in turn becomes impotent.

Angela had been married eight months when she made an appointment at her local birth control clinic. She went to see the clinic doctor, and let him know by her manner that, because of her training as a nurse, she knew just as much about the subject as he did. She discussed different contraceptive methods glibly. But when the doctor came to examine her and instruct her how to fit a diaphragm, she fainted. Later, she explained with great difficulty and many tears that she had never been able to allow her husband to make love to her. Her confident "I am in charge" manner toward the doctor turned out to be the attitude that she also took wtih her husband. She was totally unable to allow herself to be emotionally dependent on him, as she felt she would

be if he made love to her. After undergoing psychiatric treatment, she was able to recognize her own aggressive desire to control others, which she learned to curb. Later, she and her husband started a satisfactory sex life, that grew into true enjoyment.

One of the problems women have in building a happy sexual life is that the female has to cultivate sensuality. The human race could not continue without the male orgasm. It is a biological necessity, but it is also automatically pleasurable for men. On the other hand, pleasure for the woman is a luxury. Nature has equipped women for the possibility of pleasure with the clitoris, which is a unique organ of sexual satisfaction; but even if a woman never has an orgasm, or never feels pleasure, she can still conceive.

In some cases, a woman may need to learn how to relate to a man, and how to accept the feeling of dependence that love often brings, before she can really enjoy sex with him. In other cases, she may have to learn how to accept her own body without any feelings of repulsion. To help her to this, one of the most valuable and practical lessons of all might be for her to learn how to masturbate. It has been statistically demonstrated that orgasm is reached 95 per cent of the time by any woman who learns how to stimulate herself. Once she has come to know what orgasm feels like, she is more easily able to help her husband bring her to it—at first perhaps by his stimulating her with his fingers, but eventually by stimulation with his penis.

Although total satisfaction in lovemaking is always an extra for a woman, we regard it today as a necessary extra. Yet it must be remembered that sensual love is not simply a crude question of counting orgasms. It is also a question of a rich experience and close communication between two people who care about each other, and who try to please each other with their bodies as well as in all other ways. Sometimes it happens that after years of successful lovemaking the sexual side of a marriage goes flat. The wife no longer enjoys her husband's approaches. She seldom, if ever, experiences an orgasm, and she gets minimal satisfaction from helping him toward his own climax. The whole thing has become a bore. She worries about what has caused this state of affairs. Has she become frigid? Has she stopped loving her husband?

Neither of these propositions is very likely. What is more probable is that the couple has reached a phase in their lives when routine and effort have continued for too long. She and her husband may have been too responsible for too many years, earning money, looking after the children, facing up to all the pressures on them as a family. Lost in the middle of all this are the two people whose original affections for each other got the whole thing started. What often is needed is a change, a rest, a slight if temporary shedding of some of the burdens, and a chance to feel like a gay young married couple again. When life in general hits a dreary phase—in work or in the family—the sense of dreariness can infect the sexual element of the marriage. Instead of searching for aphrodisiacs, as couples used to do throughout history—and modern science has found no product that has the effect of

117

You are never too old for sex! Modern research has confirmed that men and women can continue to enjoy sexual love well beyond middle age and into their later years. In fact, 7 out of 10 couples are reported to be sexually active after age 60, and more than a few continue for a good 20 years after that. Those who keep up a regular and interesting sex life, the experts say, are the most likely to be able to go on enjoying sex for just as long as they wish.

enlivening sexual desire—the thing to search for is renewed health in mind and body, a little relaxation, a little change. Of course having a sympathetic partner helps.

It is important to check any slide into sexual inertia in time. One of the most important findings of modern research into our sexual lives has established that men and women can continue to enjoy sensual love well into old age, provided that they keep up a steady, active interest in making love. Contrary to the old myth that a man or woman must not "use themselves up" sexually in their early years, modern science has confirmed that those who keep in practice can best keep it up into old age. In other words, the more you make love, the more chance you will have of enjoying it into middle and old age. As in any other aspect

of life, the individual's whole attitude is what determines the outcome—in this case, whether sex continues to bring satisfaction into the 60's and 70's, or whether it subsides much sooner. Once a man and woman tell themselves that they are too old, they tend to become too old—for anything, not just for sex.

Doctors, social workers, and marriage counselors receive numerous complaints that either a husband or wife suddenly decides that sex has come to an end at the age of about 55. The distressed individuals themselves are uncertain whether they should still want sex or not "at their age." Doctors and counselors have, in the past, been less than sure of what to say. As for the attitude of the grown-up children of parents with sexual and marriage problems, it was too

often a shrug that indicated "they ought to know better."

Betty and Henry were in their middle 50's when their long and happy marriage hit a crisis. Betty had stopped menstruating two years before, and although she came through the menopause with good spirit, she, like many women, found it a time when she gave a lot of thought and effort to reassessing her life. Partly because their youngest son was a dropout from college, her reassessment took a gloomy turn. She began to feel that her life was pretty much past, and that it had been none too successful. All she had to look forward to was a sexless old age.

Her husband, Henry, was bewildered and upset by this change in his usually resilient wife. Finally, he went to see his doctor to discuss the situation. He told the doctor that Betty accused him of trying to be "young and foolish", but he was afraid that she had settled for a long wait for death. His doctor told Henry that sexual desire is still as normal, healthy, and essential to a man and woman in middle age as earlier. The doctor advised Henry to get his wife away for a long holiday, and to talk to her in cheerful terms about all the things they could look forward to doing together after his retirement. Once her appetite for life itself returned, so would her sexual desire. Sensual love is by no means the prerogative of youth, the doctor assured him.

Modern research into the whole subject of aging has allowed doctors and counselors to be more confident in reassuring patients in middle and old age that the normal course is for them to continue with their sexual lives for as long as they feel like it, and to encourage them to go on feeling like it by keeping up regular lovemaking. One problem that has been uncovered, however, is that a husband's sexual drive begins to subside a little more rapidly than that of his wife. Often a partnership that had problems in its early days because the husband wanted to make love more frequently than the wife, may change in the late 50's or early 60's into one in which the wife is the more sexually driven. She just has to learn to be as tolerant and undemanding at that age, as she wanted her husband to be when they were young together. They can also get around the problem by increasing the amount of time spent in sexual foreplay together and decreasing the amount of lovemaking that calls for the husband's erect penis inside her body. It is a comforting fact that by the age of 70, only 27 per cent of men in the United States have lost their sexual potency. Probably this figure is improving all the time, as older people more and more realize that it is perfectly normal for them to make love all their life.

Even the most problem-free sex lives can be further improved with a little encouragement, and encouragement is the keynote of most of the modern research by experts in the field of sex. Such research has been one of the most daring contributions of science in this country. Time and again, the old myths that bred anxiety and led people to believe that they could not achieve fulfillment in sensual love, have been dispelled. In their place has come the knowledge that sexual performance and pleasure is much easier and more delightful than they ever dreamed.

120

The Art of Loving
8

Whatever else the middle years of our century are remembered for—sending a man to the moon, or linking the world by means of the television set—it is certain that generations ahead will look back and see us also as the age that rediscovered and redefined the power of sexual love. Many critics of modern life, glancing at current bookstalls and movie posters, have decided that we are a civilization already in decadence, given over to luxurious pleasures of which uninhibited sex is the most fearful. A more sympathetic glance at our present times would perhaps assure modern men and women that, although our sexual attitudes have become permissive, and our search for sexual enjoyment more open, this is happily only one more sign of modern daring. For the first time ever, men and women have dared to look hard at human sexuality as a science, removing the myth and conjecture that obscured and tainted what happened between men and women sexually.

Sexual research can be said to have started with Kinsey, who had the courage to go out and ask people directly, for the first time, what their sexual lives were like. The most famous researchers today are Masters and Johnson, who for the first time have observed and analyzed in the laboratory what actually happens to the human body during sexual intercourse. As a result of the past 25 years of research, men and women today are the first ever to have been presented with the full "facts of life". As with any adolescent who experiences a trauma when given the details of sex for the first time, we adults can also find it a traumatic experience, and one that takes some time to get into focus.

Because we are surrounded with knowledge that is new, with research work that would have been unheard of in the past, and with general everyday discussion of sexual matters that would once have been forbidden, we think we have grown up sexually. This is not necessarily true. We have been given the signposts that should lead us to maturity in sexual matters, but finding our way to a road that leads not just to sexual experience, but also to human happiness, is the difficult task that is still left. What we have to do with all this new knowledge and frank discussion is to get it into proportion. Otherwise we are like the young woman discussed in the last chapter—she who could talk glibly about contraception in relation to sex, but who could not make sex a part of her life.

To be well informed is not the same thing as to be mature. To have learned all about sex is not the same thing as to have fallen in love. At the present, love seems to come as the greatest shock and surprise to many young people. One woman executive, who leads a well-known chain of fashion stores, has watched with fascination the love lives of the numerous young girls she employs. They are know-it-alls about sex. "But when love hits them, it bowls them over completely, and they just lose their heads", she says. The difference between second-hand knowledge of sex from manuals, or second-hand descriptions of love from novels, and the first-hand experience of love and sex is vast. In the end, what we know best is what

Others may give you all the facts you need to know about sex—but only you can learn the art of loving.

we have experienced ourselves. Nevertheless, the new discoveries and the new knowledge about sex do influence the way people behave. In the face of modern knowledge of the way women respond sexually, it is not possible for men still to maintain that there "are two kinds of women". Masters and Johnson have shown that women vary infinitely in their sexual responses, but that they are nearly all capable of enjoying sex and reaching orgasm. Refinement does not come in to it.

What does come in to it, however, is how any woman then chooses to live with the knowledge of her sexual capacity. Is she influenced to make love before marriage merely by the surveys showing that some sexual experience in early years helps her to a satisfying sexual life later? Or is she influenced by whether she meets a man she loves enough to want to make love to? In the second case, having made love to him, is her anxiety eased by knowing that a fair

Left: falling in love may bring a new delight in beauty, new feelings and new longings. With the deepening of that love, sex may also take on a new meaning, uniting all the spiritual and physical yearnings of two people within the act of love.

Below: the god of love in Greek mythology was Eros, who became Cupid in Roman mythology. Both cultures depicted him as a beautiful young boy. The idea of turning Cupid into a fat cherub came later.

proportion of other women have done this too, and found it did them as much good as—if not more good than—harm?

No woman should attempt to live her life according to a blueprint she thinks modern science has set out, and modern society accepted. She is an individual. Her life, and the love she feels for whoever she marries and makes love to, will be quite different from anyone else's. But having lived some of her life, she may be helped to see where she fits into the general pattern of human experience and human love, by reading what the experts say.

Her one aim should be to prevent the most central pleasure of her life—sensual love—from becoming dominated by lessons from modern investigations into sexual technique. She must keep first things first. In the beginning, the important point is the love and desire she feels for a man, whether he is husband or lover. To help her express that love, to increase her capacity to respond to his affection, she can turn to modern advice about sexual skills. If all she has, however, is the knowledge of the techniques to arouse and satisfy a man, she will possibly perform competently, but probably will get no self-fulfillment out of it. What is important is not mere skill in lovemaking, but the whole art of loving another human being.

The art of loving is a much more complicated matter than the skill of lovemaking, and one that takes every ounce of human energy and concentration to achieve successfully. The world is littered with people who were not able to love enough, who were not able to understand the rewards and pleasures of being intimate with another person, and wanting only good for that other person. From time to time, many marriages are afflicted by temporary sexual problems, but these can frequently be overcome (see Chapter 7), and new ways to physical pleasure discovered. It is probably safe to say that all marriages experience at least one crisis of love in a lifetime, one period in which each or both partners suddenly feels as if the other were a complete stranger. The husband that a woman may have thought of as superhumanly strong turns out to be humanly weak in some aspect of his character. The woman who appears to be flutteringly incapable and dependent, turns out to be tough and implacable in some unexpected way. They both stand exposed as a surprise and disappointment to each other. How well each of them reacts to this situation will determine the real quality of their marriage. If husband and wife prove capable of adjusting to the real person they are married to, and of recognizing that this other person is separate, "other", and always mysterious, their marriage will have survived and become stronger.

They will surely learn at the same time that a crucial way of expressing their affection and understanding of this partner, of reaching out to this other half of the twosome, is through the powerful line of communication that is proved by sex.

Frank, free, and confident, the modern woman is aware of her sexuality and equipped with the knowledge she needs to gain pleasure from her sexual life. But technique and skill in lovemaking alone may not bring her fulfillment if she does not learn to love. For it is loving deeply— caring, respecting, sharing, and wanting only good for the person one loves—that can bring the far richer rewards of true human happiness.

Words are frequently inadequate for expressing the subtle and complicated feelings between a man and woman inside a marriage. In making love, an infinitely more direct way of communication is found.

It is partly because their sensuality is to them their most honest means of direct expression that many people are worried, and put off the thought of developing sexual skills. It seems to them a corruption of what should be straightforward and spontaneous. By the same token, it seems to many that to study sexual behavior in the laboratory is almost sacreligious, exposing as it does the most private acts to a scientist's scrutiny.

This brings us back to the basic conflict that is so difficult to resolve about sex. Sex is an experience that is at once emotional and spiritual, a channel for all the most profound feelings between a man and a woman—and an experience that depends on a man's knowledge of and skill in stimulating the woman's clitoris. Mind and body are both in it, sometimes in a seemingly ludicrous way. Sex is not about technique, but it needs technique. Love and good intentions are not enough, but their presence adds greatly to the possibility of fulfillment in sex.

To read a book on sensual love is not the same as picking up a book on how to play golf. It is not possible to learn a great deal about how to be loving and desired from the printed page. Sex is not simply a modern accomplishment to be treated as a hobby. It is a central part of human happiness, and the core of a happy marriage. It is more art than sport, and consequently takes more development. The time and effort applied to cultivating sensuality can bring a reward as deep and meaningful as any in life.

Questions & Answers

Today we are inundated with information about sex. Books and magazines pour off the presses telling us how to do it, how not to do it, how often to do it, when, where—and even with whom—to do it. Movies and plays show us how other people do it. Newspapers conduct polls on it, and computer programmers juggle with statistics on it. It seems that by now we must know all there is to know about sex. But do we?

Take four women who visited a well-known doctor in the course of a single week. Betty, who is pregnant, is too scared to make love with her husband for fear of harming her baby. Julie finds intercourse painful and is afraid that she is "built too small" to enjoy a normal sex life. Rosemary is miserable because she doesn't have an orgasm each time she has intercourse, and she fears that she is frigid. Jenny is aghast to find that she is expecting a baby because she thought she couldn't become pregnant during her period. The problems of these women reveal only too clearly how myths and misconceptions about sex continue to cause much needless anxiety and unhappiness. Sometimes these misunderstandings are the result of the lingering fears and inhibitions of the past. Sometimes they are the direct result of the modern emphasis on sexual standards, formulas, and goals that can make anyone feel inadequate.

In the following pages, you will find questions and answers that examine some of the most widely believed myths—old and new—about sex. Here are straightforward answers and practical advice on some of the questions women find most difficult to ask about sex: about orgasm, masturbation, sexual desire, and painful intercourse; about sex during pregnancy; about the sexual behavior of your children and their attitudes toward sex; about venereal diseases.

Of course, no set of questions and answers could possibly cover all the individual problems that a woman might encounter in her sex life. If difficulties occur, the wise course is to seek expert advice so that problems or worries do not prevent you from the full enjoyment of the sexual side of love.

A happy, harmonious partnership forms the basis of a warm and loving family life. If parents set an example of devotion and understanding, children will learn the value of love in a relationship.

129

Some General Questions

How often should an average woman be able to experience orgasm?

No one can say. For, while every woman has the physical potential to reach orgasm whenever she wishes, the psychological factors that affect sexual pleasure make it impossible to predict how often any particular woman will do so. Research into the frequency of orgasm in women is therefore limited, but it seems certain that few women reach orgasm every time they have intercourse. It is estimated that most women have orgasms only occasionally during intercourse, but probably reach orgasm more often during sexual stimulation before or after intercourse. Women who masturbate nearly always experience orgasm during masturbation. A few women have orgasms only three or four times in their lives, and others never experience it at all.

How many consecutive orgasms can a woman have?

There is apparently no limit to the number of orgasms a woman can have. Instances of 50 consecutive orgasms in one hour have been recorded in the laboratory. Other experiments have shown that many women of all ages can regularly have five or six full orgasms within a matter of a few minutes. There may be a series of small orgasms, or one or several intense orgasms, but they follow each other in such rapid succession that, to the woman concerned, they often feel more like one continuous climax. However, multiple orgasms—or any orgasm—is not always easy to achieve during lovemaking, and it is important to remember that sex is not some kind of competition in which

multiple orgasms score more points. A happy and loving sexual relationship finds its measure in quality, not quantity.

Can a man tell if a woman has had an orgasm or not?

Orgasm can vary in intensity all the way from a mild feeling of relaxation to an extreme state of ecstasy, and there is probably no accurate way in which a man can be sure that a woman has had an orgasm. Although certain physiological changes occur in a woman's body during sexual response, these are not always readily detectable and cannot be regarded as "proof" of orgasm. This is probably just as well. The very fear of being checked for genuine responses, and maybe not matching up, is likely to make orgasm impossible for most women. The very best way in which a woman can let a man know she has had an orgasm is to tell him so herself, either by a look or gesture, or in words.

Is it true that a woman can reach orgasm more quickly by masturbating than during intercourse?

Yes. Surveys have shown that, on average, it takes only three or four minutes for a woman to reach orgasm during masturbation. During foreplay or intercourse, it normally takes considerably longer. This is probably because a woman masturbating alone is able to concentrate exclusively on her own sensations, and can control the kind and level of stimulation exactly to suit her needs.

Because masturbation can help a woman learn about her body's sexual responses in a relaxed and private atmosphere, it is sometimes advised as a temporary measure to help women who are unable to reach orgasm during intercourse—provided it causes no feelings of guilt. Masturbation is a natural and harmless outlet for sexual tension, especially at times when intercourse is impossible, but some women do not feel the need to masturbate. They should not worry about *not* masturbating any more than they should about doing it.

Is it possible for a woman to have a satisfactory sex life without experiencing orgasm?

This is a question that the woman concerned must answer for herself. A woman who never experiences orgasm may be quite happy and contented, or she may be frustrated. A loving couple may enjoy their relationship without the woman experiencing orgasm, and be just as satisfied with their lives as those who reach orgasm regularly. So long as the woman is not overstimulated, and is content to help her husband reach orgasm, her pleasure at his enjoyment may be enough. On the other hand, knowing about pleasures of orgasm but never experiencing them can make many women feel cheated and miserable. A woman who finds herself repeatedly stimulated to the point of orgasm, but is unable to gain any release for her accumulated sexual tension, is likely to suffer physically as well as mentally. Such frustration may give rise to certain forms of pelvic pain, backache, and menstrual irregularities. If a woman is at a point of high stimulation, her husband may help her reach orgasm by continuing to caress her clitoral area. Sometimes a failure to experience orgasm may be solved by the woman practicing masturbation. There are countless reasons why orgasm may elude a woman,

however, and anxious striving to achieve such a climax is one of them. So if persistent failure to reach orgasm is a matter of real concern to a woman, and she and her husband cannot resolve the problem between them, they should seek advice from a doctor trained in sexual matters, or from a marriage guidance counselor.

If intercourse is painful, does this mean that the vagina is too small?

No. The vagina is an elastic passageway, capable of stretching to accommodate any size of penis, and every woman who menstruates has a vagina adequate for sexual intercourse. The commonest reason for painful intercourse is lack of natural lubrication of the vagina, usually because the woman is not sufficiently aroused and is unable to relax. Natural secretions are sometimes lessened during pregnancy. Also, washing before intercourse may remove secretions from around the vaginal entrance. In these cases, a lubricant may solve the problem. This can also help prevent any possible discomfort when the man is using a condom. Occasional pain deep inside may also mean that there is not enough relaxation to allow complete penetration.

Persistent pain is often caused by the very fear that intercourse will be painful, or that it will result in an unwanted pregnancy, or harm a baby already conceived. This apprehension causes the woman to tighten her vaginal muscles so that the man has difficulty in inserting his penis and his attempts cause the woman pain. She may then be even more afraid of pain next time she has intercourse, until tightening the muscles becomes a habit. There are other possible reasons for painful intercourse—most of which can be quite easily treated—and no woman should hesitate in seeking medical advice if she finds that she cannot have intercourse without pain.

Does the size of a man's penis make any difference to a woman's sexual satisfaction?

No. A woman's most exciting sexual sensations are centered on the clitoris, which enlarges as the woman becomes aroused. During intercourse, the clitoris is stimulated by the movements of the penis in the vagina, which pull and release the lesser lips to which the hood of the clitoris is attached, and by contact with the man's pubic bone. All this will happen whether the man has a small penis or a large one.

The fact that penis size has nothing to do with a man's sexual capacity has not prevented researchers from delving into the question.

Recent findings are that the average non-erect penis is about 3 to $3\frac{1}{2}$ inches long and 3 inches in circumference. A penis that is small when non-erect increases in size far more than a large one, often more than doubling its length. Differences in penis size thus tend to even out after erection, and the average erect penis measures between $5\frac{1}{2}$ and $6\frac{1}{2}$ inches long, with a circumference of 4 to 5 inches. There are, of course, many variations—all perfectly normal—and penis size bears no relation whatever to body build, fertility, or a propensity to father large babies.

Can a woman ever become pregnant if the man ejaculates outside the vagina?
Yes, even if a man withdraws his penis before ejaculation, some seminal fluid may already have leaked out into the vagina and may cause pregnancy. Even if no semen is released in the vagina but the man ejaculates close to the vaginal entrance, there is still a chance of pregnancy. This is a risk even when the girl's hymen is still intact, since there is an opening in the hymen through which it is possible for the sperm to pass.

Is it true that a woman's sexual desire varies at different times in the month?
Yes, it does. Many women find that their sexual desire is intensified just before, during, or just after a period. In others, premenstrual tension before a period may lessen sexual desire. Some women are more easily aroused at midcycle. The pattern varies from one woman to another, and sometimes from month to month in the same woman.

Is it harmful to have intercourse during menstruation?
No. Provided it causes no discomfort to the woman and both partners wish it, there is no medical reason to stop having intercourse during menstruation. The vagina and other sexual organs are no more fragile than usual during a period and will not be harmed by intercourse, nor will menstrual blood cause any irritation or infection in the man. Intercourse at this time may lead to an increased menstrual flow, but during intercourse the flow normally slows down. Women who use a diaphragm will find that this can hold at least 12 hours menstrual flow. It is important to remember that you can become pregnant during menstruation, and couples who do not wish to conceive should use their usual method of birth control.

Is it true that sex can help you slim?
Yes, insofar as it provides excellent exercise. Intercourse not only tones up muscles and improves circulation but it is estimated to use up around 150 calories each time—about the equivalent of half-an-hour jogging, or an hour of hand washing and ironing.

Is sex dangerous for people with heart trouble?
It is rare for people to suffer heart attack as a result of sexual intercourse, but sexual activity does raise blood pressure and increase heart rate considerably. That is why doctors usually suggest postponing intercourse for at least two or three months after a heart attack. On the other hand, the strain and anxiety that a heart sufferer may feel if forced to abstain from sexual activity can also be dangerous. It is therefore important for those with a weak heart to be sure to consult a doctor about when and how often they may safely have sex.

132

Sex and Pregnancy

Does a woman's sexual desire decrease during pregnancy?

Sexual desire, like so many other feelings, has its ups and downs during pregnancy. A study made by William Masters and Virginia Johnson showed a general tendency for sexual appetite to increase during the third to sixth months and to decrease during the last three months. Many women, and men, are anxious about harming the baby during intercourse, and this may lessen sexual desire. Some women find that they do not wish to make love at all for short or long periods. On the other hand, couples who have previously been inhibited by contraception, or the fear of pregnancy, often find that sex becomes freer and more enjoyable, especially during the early months of pregnancy.

It sometimes happens that the vagina lubricates less easily during pregnancy, making intercourse painful. In this case, using a lubricant can help. During the second half of pregnancy, any strong pressure on the abdomen is likely to feel uncomfortable, and it is advisable to choose an alternative position for intercourse. This could be a side position with husband and wife facing each other, or with the man behind the woman, for example.

When should a pregnant woman stop having intercourse?

Recent findings suggest that it is safe to have intercourse throughout a normal pregnancy, right up until the beginning of labor. But most doctors advise stopping intercourse for about four to six weeks before the baby is due. This is just in case any germs from the outside should find their way to the uterus and cause infection during delivery. There is no need to worry that the movements of the penis in the vagina, or the contractions of the uterus during orgasm, will hurt the baby, who is well insulated inside a protective bag of watery fluid in the uterus. Also, there is no evidence that intercourse will bring on labor or increase the risk of miscarriage during the early months of pregnancy. However, if you have any cramps or bleeding during intercourse, or if you have any reason to suspect that the water may have broken, you should report this to your doctor at once and postpone further intercourse until you have his advice.

If your doctor has warned you that you might have a miscarriage, you should avoid intercourse or masturbation, as, in this case, orgasm could bring on a miscarriage. Doctors also warn against oral sex during pregnancy because of the remote but dangerous possibility that air blown into the vagina could reach the uterus and endanger the lives of both baby and mother.

It is important to ask your doctor about intercourse during your pregnancy and to be guided by his advice.

How soon can intercourse be resumed after childbirth?

Traditionally, doctors have suggested waiting until the postnatal examination about six weeks after the baby's birth; but most doctors now agree that, provided intercourse does not cause pain, it is quite safe to resume it just as soon as you feel ready to. Most women find that this is around three to six weeks after the birth. Some women prefer to wait until the *lochia* (the discharge from the uterus that normally lasts for about three to five weeks) has ceased, although this fluid is quite harmless. There is very little risk of intercourse causing infection in the early weeks after the birth, and the cervix (neck of the uterus), although still tender, cannot be harmed. You may notice some slight bleeding after intercourse at first, but this is nothing to worry about. Any tear or cut made in the vaginal opening during delivery will heal up in about three weeks, but will probably stay tender for up to six weeks. During this time, intercourse may be too painful, but a side position can sometimes be more comfortable.

In this case, too, a small amount of bleeding is no cause for alarm.

Most women feel apprehensive on first resuming intercourse, and, for this reason, the vagina often lubricates less easily. This is likely to make intercourse painful, and it is a good idea to use a lubricant until things get back to normal. It is, of course, best to proceed slowly and gently at first. However, if you find intercourse extremely painful at first, or if you are still experiencing some pain later than a month after resuming intercourse, you should consult your doctor about the matter.

Does childbirth stretch the vagina and make intercourse less satisfying?

The walls of the vagina are elastic, and although they stretch considerably during childbirth to allow the baby to pass through, the vagina is able to shrink back to its pre-pregnancy size. In most women, however, the vagina will remain slightly larger after childbirth. (Even in women who don't have children, some stretching occurs naturally as a result of repeated intercourse and the use of tampons.) This will make no difference to the woman's, or the man's, pleasure during intercourse. The size of her vagina does not affect a woman's ability to reach orgasm, and, as far as the man is concerned, it is not so much the size of the vagina as the muscles that surround it which count. These muscles, known as *levators*, are also stretched during labor, and so it is wise to exercise them regularly after childbirth to help them regain their strength. To do this, you simply contract the muscles by trying to pull the vagina and anus up inside you. Tighten the muscles as strongly as you can for about 10 seconds before letting go. You can start doing this exercise as soon as any tenderness from a tear or stitch has worn off, and you should repeat it about 50 or more times a day over the next three months. Many doctors advise practicing this exercise during late pregnancy, too, so as to keep the levators in good tone and make it easier for them to contract after the birth. Tightening the muscles regularly in this way can also help combat any tendency toward prolapse of the uterus or vagina, and some doctors suggest that all women make this exercise a daily habit whether pregnant or not.

How soon should periods resume after pregnancy?

No one can say for certain, as this varies considerably from one woman to another. If you do not nurse your baby, you will probably begin menstruating sometime between four to ten weeks after delivery, but your period could be delayed for as long as six months or more. In nursing mothers, the first period will probably not occur for about 24 weeks, and, as a rule, menstruation does not resume as long as the baby is still being breastfed. However, even nursing mothers may start menstruating as early as eight weeks, or any time after that. If your periods do start during nursing, this will not affect the quality of your milk, and you can continue breastfeeding as usual.

Can I become pregnant again before my periods resume?

Yes, you can. Remember, ovulation occurs two weeks before the first period, and you may ovulate as early as two or three weeks after delivery. Although most nursing mothers do not ovulate for about five months after childbirth, quite a number do. So, whether you are nursing your baby or not, it is wise to use a reliable method of contraception as soon as you start having intercourse again. Your postnatal examination is a good time to raise any queries you may have about birth control.

How soon can I start taking the pill again?

If you are not nursing your baby, your doctor may prescribe the pill as early as one or two weeks after the birth, but many doctors suggest waiting until the first period occurs. Nursing mothers should not take the pill for the first few weeks after giving birth, as it may cause the milk supply to dry up. This is less likely to happen once breastfeeding is well established, and some doctors will prescribe the pill during the postnatal visit about six weeks after the birth. Other doctors are more cautious because of the possible continued influence of the pill on milk production, and the fact that small amounts of hormones from the pill will reach the baby through the milk. These doctors advise women not to start on the pill again until after weaning, usually around four to six months after the birth.

Is there any way of knowing the sex of my baby before it is born?

At present, there is only one possible way of determining the sex of an unborn baby. This is by taking a sample of the fluid that surrounds the baby in the uterus and contains some of its castoff cells. These cells are then examined under the microscope, and nine times out of ten, they will reveal the sex of the baby. The fluid sample is obtained through the wall of the abdomen while the woman is under local anesthetic.

Although the risk to the mother is relatively small, doctors are unlikely to use this surgical technique simply to satisfy curiosity about the baby's sex. It is usually only done if an Rh negative blood problem is anticipated, or if some sex-linked or other rare hereditary disease is suspected.

Some women wonder if an X-ray will reveal the baby's sex. It won't. X-rays show only bones.

My first pregnancy ended in a miscarriage. Will this make me more likely to lose my next baby, too?

You have no need to worry. Your chances of having a normal pregnancy and giving birth to a healthy baby next time are just as good as if you had never had a miscarriage. While about 15 out of every 100 pregnancies sadly end in miscarriage, the vast majority of women who lose their babies in this way never had another miscarriage, no matter how many children they bear. Unlikely though it may seem to the distressed and disappointed mother, miscarriage is often a beneficial occurrence. In most cases, it happens because the fetus is defective, or is not growing properly.

Occasionally it may happen that a woman has two miscarriages in succession, but even then the following pregnancy is 75 per cent certain to be perfectly normal. Recurrent miscarriage can sometimes happen by sheer chance, but if a woman is unfortunate enough to have three or more miscarriages one after the other, her doctor is bound to insist on carrying out extensive tests to try to detect the reason. However, even after three miscarriages, a woman's chances of carrying a live, healthy baby safely to the point of delivery are still extremely high.

How long after a miscarriage is it advisable to wait before becoming pregnant again?

Some doctors advise waiting for about six months, but on the whole, this decision is up to the woman herself. Some women are anxious to become pregnant again as soon as they possibly can, and there is no medical reason to delay trying to conceive. A pregnancy that follows soon after a miscarriage is just as likely to be successful as one that comes after a considerable lapse of time. The most frequent reason for delaying a new pregnancy is an emotional one. Feelings of depression are a common reaction after miscarriage, and some women find that they have just lost interest in sex, or even develop a complete aversion to intercourse. This is a perfectly understandable phase of adjustment to the loss of a baby. It will pass with time, but it does help if you can discuss your feelings with your husband and sympathetic friends. If the problem still doesn't seem to be clearing up, it is wise to consult your doctor.

My first baby was born by a Caesarean operation. Does this mean that I must have all my babies this way, and is there a limit to the number of Caesarean operations a woman may have?

A Caesarean section is only carried out if there is some reason why the baby cannot be born through the vagina in the normal way. Whatever the reason was in your case, there is probably no way of knowing if it will recur next time you have a baby. If it does not, it is quite possible that you will be able to have a normal delivery. A recent survey made in Britain showed that 45 out of 100 women who had previously been delivered by Caesarean section had a normal vaginal delivery for a subsequent baby. However, a lot may depend on the attitude of your doctor, for some doctors will repeat the Caesarean section for all subsequent deliveries as a matter of course.

As many as 7 out of every 100 babies are born this way in the United States, and there is no limit to how many Caesarean sections a woman may have. In fact, one obstetrician reports the case of a woman who had 12 babies this way.

How do pregnancy tests work, and are they always accurate?

Pregnancy tests depend on the detection of a hormone known as HCG that is present in the urine of pregnant women. In one type of test, a sample of urine is injected into a laboratory animal, such as a mouse, toad, frog or rabbit. If the urine contains HCG, this hormone will cause the animal to ovulate. However, this test takes a few days to give results. It has mostly been superseded by a simpler chemical test in which a drop of urine is mixed with certain substances that will indicate the presence or absence of HCG in two minutes.

Both biological and chemical tests can detect pregnancy as early as three weeks after conception—about one week after the first missed period—and they are 95 per cent accurate. Occasional mistakes can occur if not enough HCG is present in the urine at the time of the test, or if there is a technical error in the laboratory. So one negative test does not absolutely rule out the possibility of pregnancy. On the other hand, one positive test is all it takes to verify pregnancy.

How can I figure out when my baby is due?

The average pregnancy lasts for 38 weeks from conception to delivery, and you can work out when your baby is likely to be born by counting 9 calendar months and 7 days (or 280 days) from the first day of your last period. Of course, this is only an approximate guide, since it is quite normal for pregnancy to be shorter or longer than 38 weeks. However, this calculation is accurate to within two weeks for four out of every five women. To avoid mistakes, it is a good idea for women to keep a systematic note of the dates of their periods, so that when they become pregnant, the doctor can calculate the date of expected birth more accurately.

Is it true that women are less likely to conceive after the age of 30?

Fertility does decline with increasing age, but this is a gradual process. It accelerates slightly not at 30, but after the age of 25.

This is true for men as well as women. However, until the woman reaches the age of about 38, when she is likely to ovulate less regularly, a couple's chances of having a baby are not substantially reduced if they continue to have intercourse fairly frequently.

What is the "safest" age at which to have a family?

According to surveys carried out in many different countries, women between the ages of 18 and 25 stand the best chance of having problem-free pregnancies and deliveries. Women under 18 or over 30 may encounter more complications during pregnancy, and those over 30 are likely to have a longer labor than their younger sisters. So, although many women outside the 18 to 25 age group do, of course, go through pregnancy and childbirth without any trouble, it is wise for younger and older mothers to obtain prenatal care as early as possible in pregnancy. Remember, too, that many factors apart from age affect each individual pregnancy. There is really no "safe" age for having a baby. The best time is when a couple decide they want one.

How long should a couple continue trying to have a baby before seeking medical advice on infertility? How long will it take to know if they can have a child?

Most doctors advise a couple to seek medical advice after trying to conceive for one year, or for six months if they are over 30. Medical examination usually takes about five visits to the doctor over a period of at least two months, although often a woman can have a number of tests done during a two-day stay in the hospital. Usually the man is examined first because tests on him are more straightforward. It is estimated that at least one couple in 20 have trouble conceiving, and the cause is just as likely to be some disorder in the man as in the woman. In about half the cases there is some factor affecting both partners. In some cases, of course, there is nothing seriously wrong and

the problem rights itself quite naturally— sometimes before the fertility study is complete. Of the apparently infertile couples who require treatment, about 35 per cent succeed in having a child.

Is it true that very frequent intercourse can actually reduce the chances of pregnancy?

Yes, if a couple has intercourse too often before ovulation, this may diminish the supply of sperm available to fertilize the egg, even though the amount of semen released appears to be the same as usual. In addition, if a couple is anxiously trying to conceive, the resulting tension can in itself lessen the chances of pregnancy.

What sort of exercise should I take during pregnancy?

It is important to take plenty of exercise during pregnancy. Any kind of exercise is good, provided it is not overstrenuous or exhausting. You can swim, dance, play tennis or golf, walk, or garden, as long as you enjoy it and feel able to do it. There is no reason at all to change your normal activities, especially if they include regular exercise.

How can I prevent stretch marks developing during pregnancy?

Try massaging your abdomen, breasts, and thighs once or twice a day with oil or moisturizing cream. This is not guaranteed to prevent the marks, but it will certainly help to keep your skin supple. Stretch marks are partly due to the amount of elasticity in your skin, and partly to the hormones present during pregnancy. After pregnancy, they will fade away naturally.

Sex and Your Child

At what age does a child normally start to have sexual feelings?
Children have sexual feelings from the time they are born. These are not, of course, as powerful as the sexual feelings of an adult, and they are not necessarily centered on the sexual organs. Nevertheless, it is common for baby boys to have an erection, and both male and female babies soon discover, quite by chance, that pleasurable sensations come from touching their sexual organs, or maybe rubbing them against the sides or mattress of their cot. This early form of masturbation is as common and normal as thumb-sucking, and is part of a child's natural development.

Do all children masturbate?
Most babies—girls as well as boys—probably masturbate to some extent. Some babies don't. A baby who doesn't masturbate seems to develop sexually just as well as a baby who does.

Although masturbation is common in infancy and early childhood, it occurs less frequently in the 6 to 10 age group, and then normally starts again during puberty. Well over half of all boys resume masturbation between the ages of 10 and 13, and almost all boys are masturbating by the age of 16. For girls, the picture is different. It is estimated that probably only half of all adolescent girls masturbate. Of these, some begin as early as age 8, and most have begun by the age of 15. After adolescence, however, masturbation is commoner in women than in men.

If I find my child masturbating, how should I react?

Don't react. Continue whatever you were doing, as though you hadn't noticed. Masturbation is as normal a part of a child's behavior as eating or playing, and it is important not to make it seem unnatural or wrong. Any expression of disgust or disapproval, or attempts to restrain or punish the child, may harm his sexual adjustment in later years.

There's no reason to go to the other extreme though. Parents who find their adolescent child masturbating and exclaim in approval and encouragement are just as likely to cause harm as those who appear shocked. Masturbation is a private affair, so don't draw attention to it. Just leave well enough alone.

What if my child masturbates in front of guests, or in public?
In this case, it is probably best to try to distract the child's attention as gently as possible. Try not to appear alarmed or embarrassed, and restrain the impulse to pull the child's hand away, or to place him firmly in a position in which he can no longer enjoy himself. Instead, try as naturally as you can to get him interested in something else.

Is it true that the way in which a child

is toilet trained influences his or her attitude toward sex in later life?

Yes, it is. Excessive strictness in toilet training can sometimes lead to sexual inhibition later in life. Because the sexual and excretory organs are so close together, a child is likely to link the two functions in its mind. Most children naturally go through a phase during which they are fascinated by their own excreta. Passing water and moving their bowels is a satisfying achievement, and they are proud of the results. If the parents react with disgust at what the child has produced, he may get the idea that this whole area of his body is in some way dirty and unpleasant.

Hard though it may be, parents should try to be calm and patient over toilet training. You should encourage the child to use the pot regularly, but let him take his time over it. Appear interested in what the child is doing, and pleased if he produces something. If nothing happens, don't show disappointment, and never scold or punish the child for this. Don't worry if your child is slow in adopting good toilet habits. This varies from child to child, and has nothing to do with backwardness in other respects.

At what age should a child be told the "facts of life", and what is the best way of giving this information?

The best time to tell children about sex is when they ask about it. Their questions should be answered simply and naturally as soon as they are asked. Parents can then use the opportunity to give the child just as much information as seems relevant to the particular question, although they should be careful not to overburden him with a lot of facts he hasn't asked for. Once his attention wanders, it's time to stop. Other opportunities will arise.

By the time they go to school, children probably ought to have been told where babies come from, how they got there, and how they got out. Otherwise they might pick up too many misguided notions from other children. A little girl must, of course, know

about menstruation before she has her first period. (This may happen as early as age 10, possibly even before). Here again, it is best if an explanation can arise naturally, possibly in answer to a question. A mother should explain simply but accurately why menstruation happens and describe it as a perfectly normal occurrence. It is very important not to show any distaste about the subject, or to indicate that periods may be painful or unpleasant.

Is it a good idea for children to see their parents naked?

This all depends on the parents' own attitude to nudity. A child who is used to seeing his parents naked, and to being naked with them, may well develop a healthier and less inhibited attitude to sex than other children. But if parents want their child to regard nakedness as normal, they must be entirely unselfconscious about it themselves. It is no good suddenly deciding that nakedness would be a good idea when the child has not been used to this, or if the parents feel embarrassed without clothes. On the other hand, it will probably do no harm if the child comes across one or other of its parents in the bathroom, or getting dressed or undressed.

At what age is it safe for a girl to start using tampons? Is it true that if she does use them, she will no longer be technically a virgin?

Some doctors advise waiting until a girl is about 16 or 17 before she uses tampons. Others say that, as soon as a girl is old enough to have periods, she is old enough to use tampons provided she can insert them without discomfort. In most girls, the opening in the hymen through which the menstrual flow escapes is large enough to accommodate a tampon, but if a girl has difficulty in inserting a tampon, she should consult her doctor. The use of tampons may stretch the hymen — so may strenuous sports, petting, masturbation, medical examination, or even washing—but is not likely to break it.

Venereal Disease

How can a woman tell if she has VD?
There are two main venereal diseases: gonorrhea, which is usually confined to the genital organs, and syphilis, which invades the entire body. If a woman has either of these diseases, she may notice certain characteristic symptoms.

What are the symptoms of gonorrhea?
The first symptoms are a frequent desire to urinate and discomfort on passing urine, together with a discharge from the bladder, and possibly some vaginal discharge. These symptoms usually show up within five days of infection, but may not appear for as long as three weeks. Unfortunately, however, as many as four women out of five either have no symptoms whatever at this stage, or mistake the symptoms for those of some other disorder, such as cystitis.

What happens if gonorrhea is not detected at this stage?
Several other complications may occur. The glands in the genital area may swell and become painful; abcesses may develop at the opening of the vagina or bladder, possibly giving rise to painful urination; or the infection may spread to the rectum. Worst of all, the gonorrhea germs may work their way upward through the uterus to infect the Fallopian tubes (the tubes that carry eggs from the ovaries to the uterus). At this point, the woman may feel severe pain on one or both sides of her lower abdomen, possibly associated with fever and vomiting—symptoms like those of appendicitis. These symptoms may recur in a milder form over several weeks or months. The woman may also suffer from anemia or lose weight, and her periods may become irregular. If the disease is still not treated, the Fallopian tubes may eventually become scarred and blocked, so that eggs cannot travel through them. The woman is then no longer able to have children. (This happens to about 15 out of every 100 women who contract gonorrhea.)

What are the symptoms of syphillis?
The first sign is a *chancre,* or sore. This usually appears on or near the genitals, although it may occur on the mouth, breast, fingers, or anus. The chancre, which may show up at any time from 9 to 90 days after infection, usually looks like a pimple or blister, but it may appear as an open sore. A quarter of all infected women never notice this sore because it develops inside the vagina or on the cervix (the neck of the uterus), where it is completely hidden.

What happens to the sore?
It disappears of its own accord—usually after a few weeks. But the syphillis germs continue to spread through the body as the disease enters its second stage.

Are there any symptoms during this stage?

Yes. Between a few weeks and six months after the appearance of the chancre, any of a number of symptoms may occur. The commonest of these is a pink, spotty rash which may occur anywhere on the body, but is often noticed on the chest, back and arms, or on the hands and feet. The rash, although faint at first, may become coppery-red, and is usually not itchy. It is likely to persist for several weeks and may then fade and return several times over a period of months or years. Other symptoms that may occur during this stage of the disease are: sores in the mouth; sore throat; mild fever; headache; swollen glands, especially around the gentials and anus; and loss of hair in patches. Unfortunately, all these symptoms, including the rashes, may be attributed to some other minor complaint, or may be so mild as to pass almost unnoticed. This stage of the disease usually lasts for three to six months, but symptoms may recur for as long as four years.

Then what happens?

All outward signs of syphilis vanish, and the disease enters a latent stage that may last for 5 to 50 years, during which the infected person feels perfectly healthy. Meanwhile, the syphilis germs may be invading the body's organs, and in the final stage of the disease, they may cause heart complaints, paralysis, blindness, or insanity. Between 25 and 30 out of every 100 untreated syphilitics are eventually killed or incapacitated by the disease. In the others, syphilis will either remain dormant for a person's lifetime, or die out.

What if a woman thinks she has VD but has no symptoms?

With or without symptoms, the only way to make sure whether or not you have VD is to go to a doctor or clinic for specialized tests. Above all, don't let feelings of shame or embarrassment prevent you from seeking medical help if you think that there is even the slightest chance that you may have caught VD.

What are the tests for VD, and are they always accurate?

Tests for gonorrhea are usually made by taking specimens of secretions from the vagina, cervix, and urethra (the exit from the bladder). Some of these samples are then examined under the microscope for gonorrhea germs, while others are kept in the laboratory for two or three days so that any germs which may be present will mutiply and become easier to identify. One set of tests is usually sufficient to detect gonorrhea in a man, but in a woman, it is often necessary to repeat the tests in order to make sure there are no germs.

There are two main tests for syphilis. If there is a chancre or a rash, the doctor may take fluid from these and examine it under the microscope. But the disease is usually detected by a special blood test. This test can reveal syphilis after the disease has been present in the body for more than five or six weeks, or about a week or two after the appearance of a chancre. Occasionally one blood test may fail to detect syphilis, and it is therefore wise to have another blood test several weeks later just to be on the safe side.

A blood test for syphilis is usually given as a matter of course to couples wishing to get a marriage license, to pregnant women, and to blood donors.

How can VD be cured, and how long does treatment take?

Both gonorrhea and syphilis can be cured by penicillin. Usually only one or two injections of penicillin are needed, although sometimes a series of injections may be given over a period of weeks. For people who are allergic to penicillin, other equally effective antibiotics can be used.

The dose required to cure syphilis is usually higher than that for gonorrhea, and, since it's quite possible for someone to have both diseases at the same time, anyone seeking treatment for gonorrhea should also have a blood test for syphilis before receiving penicillin or any other drug.

Whatever the dose prescribed, it is essential for repeated examinations and blood tests to be carried out, usually for about six months after treatment.

Is it possible to catch VD without having intercourse—from a toilet seat, or just from kissing, for example?

The germs that cause gonorrhea and syphilis depend on the warmth and moisture of the human body for survival. Once outside the body, where conditions are too cool or too dry for them, they die in a matter of seconds. This means that it is virtually impossible to catch either of these diseases from a toilet seat, towel, or cup, for example. The germs just don't live long enough. Sexual intercourse, on the other hand, provides ideal conditions for the transmission of VD germs. It is possible to catch VD during oral sex or any other intimate physical contact that enables germs to get onto warm moist surfaces—around the genitals, inside the mouth, or on a break in the skin, for instance. Contact with the sores that occur during the second stage of syphilis may be enough to spread this disease. VD may occasionally be transmitted by kissing or biting, or if germs on wet fingers are deposited on the eyes, but this doesn't happen often. Almost always, VD is caught by intercourse or genital contact with an infected person.

I am dreadfully worried that I may have caught VD, but I dare not seek treatment in case my husband finds out that I have slept with another man. Must he know?

Your first step must be to go to a VD clinic or to a doctor and find out whether you have VD. Your health—maybe even your life—is at stake. It is vital not to let any feelings of guilt or embarrassment prevent you from seeking treatment. Doctors in clinics see hundreds of people with VD every week. They are interested in curing the disease, not in passing moral judgments.

Maybe you haven't got VD, in which case the sooner you put your mind at rest the better. If you have, no one is going to tell your husband about it unless you do. A clinic will ask you for the names of your sexual contacts, so that they can be contacted and treated. Your name and theirs will be kept completely secret. Even so, you are not obliged to give this information, and no one will notify your husband if you do not wish it. However, if you reveal no names, you have a strong responsibility to inform any of your sexual contacts—including your husband. If you do not tell him, you will place his health in jeopardy, and you will, of course, also run the risk of catching the disease again from him.

I am frightened that I may have caught VD many years ago. Would it still be possible for tests to detect the disease, and would treatment still be effective after all this time?

Blood tests for syphilis will detect the disease no matter how long ago you contracted it. Treatment with penicillin or similar drugs can cure syphilis completely during the first three stages of the disease and, even during the final stage, the destructive effects of syphilis can be halted.

Gonorrhea is more difficult to diagnose at any stage, and after a number of years, germs may no longer show up in a sample of secretions from the cervix or vagina. (In some cases, the germs may even have entirely disappeared from the body by this time.) Because diagnosis is uncertain, doctors will sometimes prescribe penicillin treatment if a woman thinks there is a strong possibility that she has caught gonorrhea, even if tests are negative. Treatment will cure gonorrhea at any time, but any damage to the Fallopian tubes will remain, and may require surgery. Such damage, which is likely to cause obvious symptoms (see p. 140) can be revealed by pelvic examination. Blockage of the tubes is detected by attempting to pass carbon dioxide gas through them, a test usually made during fertility studies. Occasionally, an operation may succeed in unblocking the Fallopian tubes if the extent of the blockage is not too great.

If a woman with VD becomes pregnant, does the disease always harm her baby? Would treatment of such an expectant mother cause any damage to the baby?

An expectant mother with syphilis can pass on the disease to her unborn child. The more recently she has caught the disease, the more likely her baby is to be affected. Even if the woman has had syphilis for as long as twenty years, her baby still has one chance in six of contracting the disease in the womb. An infected baby may be miscarried, born dead or deformed, or may develop symptoms of chronic syphilis later in life. Inherited, or congenital, syphilis can be detected by blood tests and cured by penicillin, but treatment will not undo any damage that has already been done during development in the womb. It is therefore vital that all pregnant women have a blood test for syphilis early in pregnancy. Syphilis is not usually transmitted to the baby before the fourth month of pregnancy, and so the mother may be cured before the baby is infected. Even if penicillin is not given until late in pregnancy, the mother may still have a healthy baby.

Gonorrhea in an expectant mother is likely to infect her baby's eyes during the birth, and cause blindness. Nowadays, every newborn baby in the United States is given eye drops to kill any gonorrhea germs that may be present. This should not prevent any pregnant woman who thinks she may have gonorrhea from getting tests for the disease.

Penicillin treatment for gonorrhea or syphilis will not harm the baby at any time during pregnancy.

Is it true that the use of a condom will prevent a man from catching or transmitting VD, and that douching after intercourse prevents a woman from catching such disease?

Use of a condom, or douching, may lessen the risk of infection. So may washing with soap and water, or antiseptic solution, before and after intercourse. But these methods are not reliable. No matter how good your personal hygiene, you can still catch or transmit a venereal disease.

Is it possible to be exposed to VD and not catch it, or will a person with VD always infect his or her sexual contact?

During the third, or dormant, stage of syphilis (usually from about four years after infection onward), the disease is no longer infectious to a sexual partner. There is also some evidence that untreated gonorrhea becomes less infectious as time goes by. A few people, especially men, seem to be immune to VD, but people with no symptoms can still be carriers of the disease—so it's obviously not worth taking the risk.

Would a Pap smear be able to detect VD?

A Pap smear cannot detect syphilis; a blood test is needed for that. In the case of gonorrhea, a Pap smear might just reveal it if there were sufficient germs to be noticeable when the smear is examined under the microscope, but this is unlikely. Almost always, a "culture" (growth resulting from cultivation of germs in a laboratory) is necessary to detect gonorrhea. It is, of course, possible for a woman to ask her doctor to take what is called a "cervical smear and culture for GC" at the same time as she has a Pap smear. Some doctors would like to see this done regularly once a year, together with a blood test for syphilis, to protect women and help prevent the spread of VD.

Are there any other venereal diseases besides gonorrhea and syphilis?

The term venereal disease, although usually taken to mean gonorrhea and syphilis, also applies to other diseases transmitted by sexual contact. There are at least a dozen of these diseases, most of which cause abnormal vaginal discharge, itching, sores, or swellings around the genitals. Many of these are very common infections that can be easily treated, and it is wise to see your doctor at the first sign of any such symptoms.

For Your Bookshelf

Sexual Pleasure in Marriage
by Jerome and Julia Rainer, Julian Messner, Inc. (New York: 1959); Souvenir Press Ltd. (London: 1959)

Sex and the Over-Fifties
by Robert Chartham, Brandon Books Ltd. (North Hollywood: 1972);
Sex and the Over-Forties (UK title)
Leslie Frewin Ltd. (London: 1969)

Sexual Responsibility in Marriage
by Maxine Davis, Dial Press, Inc. (New York: 1963); William Heinemann Ltd. (London: 1964)

Any Woman Can!
by David Reuben M.D., David McKay Co., Inc. (New York: 1972); W.H. Allen & Co. (London: 1972)

The Complete Sex Dictionary
by Dr. Paul J. Gillette, Universal Publishing & Distributing Corp. (New York: 1969); Universal Tandem Publishing Co. Ltd. (London: 1969)

Techniques of Sexual Fitness
by James Hewitt, Universal Publishing & Distributing Corporation (New York: 1969);
Live Well, Love Better (UK title)
Universal Tandem Publishing Co. Ltd. (London: 1971)

Picture Credits